Modern Furniture in Canada
1920 to 1970

In this richly illustrated study, Virginia Wright explores the history of modern furniture in Canada, employing archival photographs and original documents to trace the development of professional design, design education, and design advocacy in the period from 1920 to 1970.

Canada has a distinguished record in modern furniture design and has produced work of international significance, some of it hitherto unrecognized. Chief among the milestones were the production in Ontario in the mid-1920s of moulded-plywood seating for assembly halls and of the world's first moulded-plastic furniture, produced in prototype by the National Research Council in 1946 – three years before the more famous designs by Charles Eames in the United States were unveiled.

Wright charts the development of modern furniture design in Canada, from its first appearance in an Eaton's department store display of pieces brought from the Paris Exposition of 1925, through its gradual entry into Canadian homes, to its establishment as a dominant style. She shows how modern industrial materials such as steel tubing, rubber, and plywood were incorporated into the production of commercial and institutional furnishings and how these designs reached a wide public through exhibitions and the media. Wright also reveals the relative neglect of this facet of Canada's art history by its museums and galleries, who, after featuring exhibits of new furniture made in Canada, failed to acquire any for their own permanent exhibitions or study collections.

The first account of Canada'a innovative furniture design and production of the period, *Modern Furniture in Canada, 1920 to 1970* opens the door to a whole new field of study.

Virginia Wright is an adjunct assistant professor in the School of Architecture and Landscape Architecture, University of Toronto, and a lecturer in the School of Crafts and Design, Sheridan College.

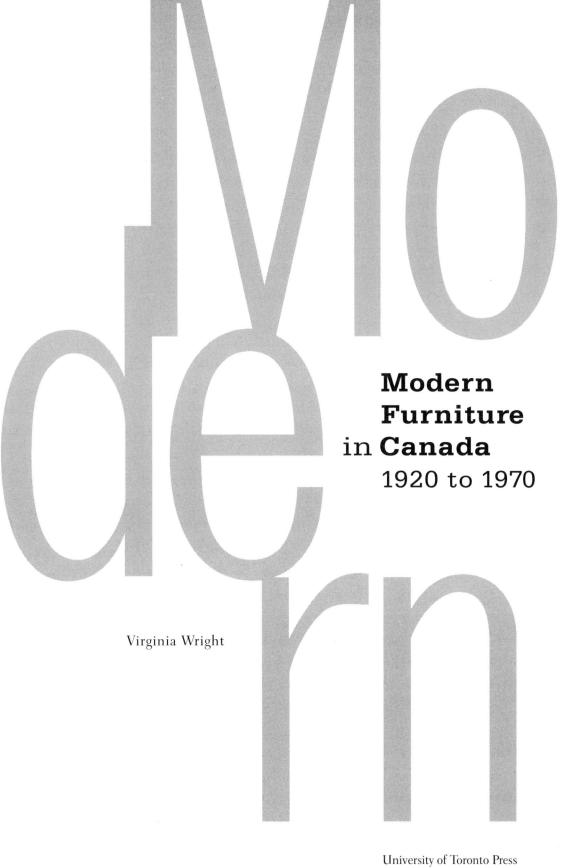

Modern
Furniture
in Canada
1920 to 1970

Virginia Wright

University of Toronto Press
Toronto Buffalo London

University of Toronto Press
Toronto Buffalo London

© University of Toronto Press Incorporated 1997
Toronto Buffalo London
Printed in Canada

ISBN 0-8020-2873-X (cloth)
ISBN 0-8020-7377-8 (paper)
∞ Printed on acid-free paper

Canadian Cataloguing in Publication Data

Wright, Virginia, 1950–
  Modern furniture in Canada, 1920 to 1970

Includes bibliographical references and index.
ISBN 0-8020-2873-X (bound)
ISBN 0-8020-7377-8 (pbk)

1. Furniture design – Canada – History – 20th
century.
I. Title.

NK2441.W75 1997   749.211   C96-930643-1

The author and University of Toronto Press
acknowledge the financial assistance of the
Canada Council and the Ontario Arts Council
in the writing and publishing of this book.

To the memory of my mother,
Molly Wright, and of her mother,
Catherine Whitnall

Contents

List of Figures and Plates

Plates

Fig. 1 Guest room, Hotel Marriaggi, Winnipeg, Manitoba, *ca* 1903 (Provincial Archives of Manitoba)

Introduction

Modern furniture expresses the art and invention of the industrial era. 'Modern' is not a style of furniture, but rather an explosion of styles ignited by the accelerating pace of industrial production and design experimentation during the nineteenth and twentieth centuries. The research associated with this growth in manufacturing created a new type of design practitioner, the professional furniture designer, able to marry the aesthetic preoccupations of art and architecture with the practical applications of new materials and production processes.

These modern designers were men and women from differing backgrounds – craftspeople, architects, decorative-arts dealers, artists, and manufacturers – who shared an impassioned interest in the furnishing of domestic and public interiors (fig.1). Their work forged a conscientious alliance between crafts and industry, developing new approaches to furniture-designing and -making that augmented traditional craft techniques with the principles and methods of mass production.

These activities, which culminated in the revolutionary furniture designs of the 1920s, were augmented by the rapid development of professional interior design during the 1930s, when art schools added furniture design and interior architecture to existing decorative-arts and decoration courses. After the Second World War, the professional range of furniture designers was further expanded when industrial design courses were introduced at art schools and universities. As a result, a diverse group of craft and design practitioners was able to meet the demands of new technologies and new markets, in Canada as elsewhere.

The chronological course of this progression is reflected in the text of this book, which looks at various aspects of furniture history in Canada between 1920 and 1970. The accompanying illustrations have been selected from national, provincial, municipal, university, corporate, and private archives across the country. They are presented within a narrative framework that traces many of the issues affecting the practice of furniture design. The book's fifty-year span encompasses the commercial birth of this field of design in Canada and its subsequent development, concurrent with the growth, and demise, of government support and public advocacy.

Modern industrial materials, such as steel tube, rubber, and plywood, were first used in the Canadian furniture industry to produce starkly plain commercial and institutional furnishings. These materials were then incorporated into a new type of glamorous modern décor that was persuasively presented in small shops and in the new department stores, where interior decorators designed impressive residential interiors for wealthy clients and inspiring retail displays for everyone else. New work by furniture makers and designers from Canada and other countries was brought to the attention of a wide public audience through increasingly frequent and popular decorative-arts exhibitions, and through magazine coverage of new products and of newly built or renovated local homes and stores.

During the Second World War, public attention shifted from these retailer/decorator teams to manufacturer/designer teams, as new government support for industrial design research moved the educational and commercial focus of furniture design from 'the setting' to 'the product.' Government-sponsored displays at international expositions, before and after the war, featured new furniture made in Canada, as did exhibitions at major museums and art galleries. These public institutions, however, did not actually acquire any of this furniture for their own permanent collections.

The designing and making of furniture is a field rich in history, complex in meaning, boundlessly alive with technical leap-frogging and aesthetic leaps of faith, yet no museum, art gallery, or exhibition centre has developed a mandate to collect, conserve, publish, and exhibit Canadian furniture of the twentieth century. Surviving pieces are scattered among private collections, and a few museum storerooms, in many cases still meeting their functional obligations and vulnerable to irreparable damage or abandonment.

Canada's furniture history includes work of international significance in the history of modern design. For example, very early compound-curve moulded plywood was used in assembly-hall seating made in Ontario in the mid-1920s (plate 1), and the world's first one-piece moulded-plastic chair was developed in Ottawa in 1946 by architects working for the National Research Council of Canada (figs.124–6). These innovations were ahead of dates currently published for the origination of these furniture design processes in the United States and Europe.

I hope that readers will enjoy and make use of the results of my ongoing research, and that professional Canadian furniture designers and makers will find inspiration in the work of their neglected predecessors, who contributed in lasting and substantive ways to the world of furniture and to the modern daily life of Canada.

Assembly Chairs for Halls

Plate 1 Chair for assembly halls. Frame: steel, black baked enamel, bolted to floor, set in circular or straight rows of three or more. Seat and back: 'compound curved five ply, cross banded veneer,' mahogany stain. Arms: wood, mahogany stain. An unusual example of early moulded-plywood furniture. Made by the Globe Furniture Company, Waterloo, Ontario, *ca* 1925. Also available with more elaborate steel frame for use in 'Sanctuary and Chancel' (Globe Furniture catalogue, *ca* 1925, Metropolitan Toronto Reference Library, Special Collections)

Plate 2 Illustration by Franklin Carmichael from 'Her Personal Car,' the Ford Motor Company, Canada, *ca* 1926 (National Archives of Canada/C130432)

Plate 3 Cover of *Canadian Homes and Gardens* magazine.
(February 1929)

Plate 4 Illustration from advertisement for Snyder's furniture. Caption: 'It was not the thing to do when I was a girl' (*Canadian Homes and Gardens*, April 1934)

Plate 5 Advertisement for furniture by the Dominion Chain Company, Niagara Falls, Ontario, and Niagara Falls, New York (*Canadian Homes and Gardens*, June–July 1934)

Plate 6 Illustration from advertisement for 'Modern Maple' living-room furniture designed by Russell Wright. Made of 'solid Canadian Rock Maple' by Snyder's, Waterloo, Ontario, and Montreal, Quebec (*Canadian Homes and Gardens*, April 1936)

Plate 7 Advertisement for Snyder's furniture
(*Canadian Homes and Gardens*, April 1950)

Plate 8 Interior of Canada's first geodesic-dome residence. Home of architect Jeffrey Lindsay, Morin Heights, Quebec. Furniture by the Herman Miller Company and others (Cover, *Canadian Homes and Gardens*, June 1953)

Modern Furniture in Canada
1920 to 1970

Definite modern

Restrained modern

Swedish modern

Modified modern

Interchangeable modern

Traditional modern

Sensible modern

Efficient modern

Informal modern

Transitional modern

Mandarin modern

Malay modern

Mexican modern

Moveable modern

Completely modern

Canadian Homes and Gardens,
1929–1955

Fig. 2 Operating theatre, Vancouver General Hospital, *ca* 1910. Furniture and fixtures in cast iron, steel, porcelain, glass, rubber (City of Vancouver Archives/99-92)

Introduction from Europe

The first types of furniture described as 'modern' in Canada were commercial and institutional, made for hospitals, clinics, schools, assembly halls, and cafeterias. They were manufactured using industrial materials, such as cast or bent steel (figs. 2–4), and new industrial processes, such as plywood moulding (plate 1). These chairs, tables, and cabinets, in durable and easily cleaned materials, were notable for their extreme functionalist efficiency. This aspect of their design formed a significant part of the products' appeal, enabling employers and educators to demonstrate admirably progressive views on health standards in workplaces and meeting-places.

British suffragist Emmeline Pankhurst reminded Canadian industrialists of their obligations in this regard when she addressed the Toronto Branch of the Canadian Manufacturers' Association in December 1921. Her lecture, which stressed the importance of staff cafeterias, was titled 'The Part that Large Employers Can Play in Making a Healthier Country,' and was presented under the auspices of the Canadian National Council for the Promotion of Social Hygiene. Pankhurst's talk spurred a great deal of advertising in Canadian trade publications by manufacturers of modern hygienic furniture and fixtures. McClary's, manufacturers of cooking and serving equipment in London, Ontario, advertised in February 1922 that 'cafeterias are becoming more of a necessity in modern Industrial Institutions every day.'[1] Gleamingly clean cafeterias and cafés were also installed in new department stores, usually in the basement, mixing the shoppers with the shop assistants on chrome-plated swivelling stools around stainless-steel embankments of coffee dispensers and pastry-display cases (fig. 5).

The Globe Furniture Company, of Waterloo, Ontario, explained in their *School Furniture* catalogue that the triangular form of steel construction used in their 'Steel Sanitary Desks'

> affords no lodgment for dust or dirt. All filigree work ... has been abandoned. The feet ... afford a close, tight-fitting, substantial joint and support on the floor. This permits no opportunity for the accumulation of dirt and bacteria. The same dust cloth used on the top will cleanse the metal work from every particle of dust.

Globe Furniture vigorously promoted the health benefits of another product, the 'Adjustable Automatic Desk,' warning that 'serious diseases of the eye, spine and lungs are the inevitable outgrowth of ill-fitting desks and seats.' The company confidently claimed that their 'School Desks, Teachers' Desks, Recitation and Lecture Room Seating, Physical and Chemical Laboratory Desks, Domestic Science Tables and Manual Training Benches are the MOST MODERN and mechanically, most perfect.'

Canadian homes were first described as 'modern' in the early 1920s, when they acquired better plumbing and more extensive electrical wiring. Advertising by utility companies showed home-buying couples and real-estate agents staring and pointing at light switches and power outlets in empty new houses. Young housewives and mothers quickly became the principal beneficiaries of local interest in new designs. Lightweight metal baby-strollers, manufactured by Gendron, in Toronto, and square wooden playpen/cribs called 'Kiddie-Koops' (fig. 6), made by Lea-Trimble Manufacturing Company, also in Toronto, were the first overtly modern products advertised in national magazines. The cribs were distinguished by their stark, delicate geometry and no-nonsense, hybrid functionalism.

The Thomas Furniture Company, in London, Ontario, boosted their business with a baby clinic (medical examination *cum* baby contest) held during their 'Baby Week' promotion in 1923. Furniture and baby-carriages were offered at 'attractive prices,' with a 'liberal payment plan,' and all babies attending received a souvenir bib.[2]

New colours and textures were introduced into the home through furnishing fabrics, patterned wallpapers and carpets (fig. 7), and bright enamel paints. Plush upholstery fabrics and sheer curtains added a layer of gossamer sheen to living rooms, dining rooms, and bedrooms. Highly reflective surfaces were admired on new types of chrome and ceramic fixtures for bathrooms (fig. 8), on painted cabinetry in kitchens (fig. 9), and on chrome-plated or enamelled metals in furniture and lighting. New bending, moulding, and casting techniques produced rounded corners and streamlined curves, while veneered wooden cabinetry emphasized intricate geometric surfaces and shapes.

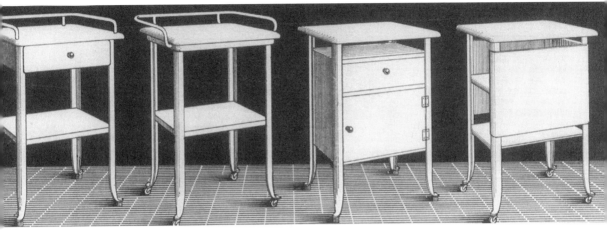

Fig. 3 Medical tables and cabinets: painted sheet steel, bent steel, steel tube. Made by Metal Craft Company, Toronto, 1927 (Metal Craft Company catalogue, Metropolitan Toronto Reference Library, Special Collections)

Fig. 4 Medical examination chair: painted steel tube and sheet steel. Made by Metal Craft Company, Toronto, 1927 (Metal Craft Company catalogue, Metropolitan Toronto Reference Library, Special Collections)

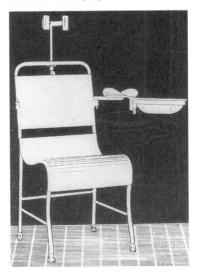

Fig. 5 Basement café of the Robert Simpson Company, Toronto, 1920. Chrome-plated steel stools made in Canada (McLaughlin Soda Fountain Company catalogue, Metropolitan Toronto Reference Library, Special Collections)

Fig. 6 Créche tent at the Canadian National Exhibition, Toronto, 1927. 'Kiddie-Koop' playpen/cribs in solid wood made by Lea-Trimble Manufacturing Company, Toronto (*Canadian Homes and Gardens*, December 1927)

Fig. 7 Guest room, Casa Loma, Toronto, *ca* 1920 (City of Toronto Archives/James 4076)

Modern decorative arts made their official entry into Canada on the morning of 5 November 1925, conveyed by the women's section of the Toronto *Globe*. A full-page advertisement for the T. Eaton Company, the country's largest chain of department stores, announced that 'this is the ferro-concrete age, the age of steel, of electricity, of motors, of aeroplanes. And with our new needs and wider outlook come a new architecture and a new style of ornament in arts and crafts.' Tasselled pillows in silk and velvet were described as having pattern as 'simple as a pattern can be' or 'intricate as a kaleidoscope device.' The wallpapers had 'new allure,' and the pottery was 'the result of a very definite attempt to evolve something new.'

Many of the items advertised had been purchased by Eaton's at the 1925 Paris exposition, l'Exposition Internationale des Arts Décoratifs et Industriels Modernes. This exposition was a milestone in the history of architecture and interior design. But the significance of the event was not anticipated by many of the dozens of countries invited to participate. The United States declined an invitation because, as Herbert Hoover, then secretary of commerce, said: 'They [American manufacturers] did not consider that we could contribute sufficiently varied design of unique character or of special expression in American artistry.'[3] The British were reluctant to exhibit, complaining in a subsequent government report that European 'customs policies were so inimical to the successful penetration of British works of industrial art into their markets' that invitations to exhibitions had become frustrating and not remunerative. Even those British manufacturers who eventually decided to participate 'failed to grasp the real significance of the Exhibition, or the vast distance which separated it from the ordinary trade fair.'[4]

The Canadian under-secretary of state for external affairs had received an invitation for Canada to participate in the exposition from the consul-general of France in Montreal, in November 1923. This invitation was passed on to the Department of Immigration and Colonization, organizers of Canadian exhibitions in England and elsewhere, who, in turn, passed it on to A.W. Tolmie, the Canadian exhibition commissioner in London. He discussed it with the Australian exhibition commissioner, who informed him that Australia was not taking part. 'It seems to me,' reported Tolmie, 'that this is purely a commercial exhibit, confined to Arts & Crafts.' He recommended that Canada wait, along with other outposts of the British Empire, for a colonial exposition that the French government was planning for 1927.

Canada had participated in many previous international expositions. For the 1924 and 1925 British Empire exhibitions at Wembley, the federal government had commissioned an extravagant pavilion called 'The Palace of Beauty,' which Queen Mary thought 'wonderful.' It featured a series of 65-foot-wide panoramas depicting the route of the Canadian transcontinental railway, from the Atlantic to the Pacific, along with displays from more than 300 manufacturers that included railway carriages and a University of Toronto stand presenting Banting and Best's new process for manufacturing insulin. Outside, there was a 400-foot-long ice toboggan slide, with six tracks that could accommodate 12,000 riders per hour. The Canadian furniture exhibition in the pavilion was not so daring. It consisted of two rooms deco-

Fig. 8 Bathroom furnishings: chrome-plated steel tube, ceramic, and mirrored glass. Made by Crane, Montreal, 1922 (Crane catalogue, Metropolitan Toronto Reference Library, Special Collections)

Fig. 9 Kitchen Maid cabinet: (a) closed. Advertisement for Aikenhead Hardware, Toronto, in *Canadian Homes and Gardens* (June 1926); (b) open. Advertisement for Aikenhead Hardware, Toronto, in *Canadian Homes and Gardens* (August 1926)

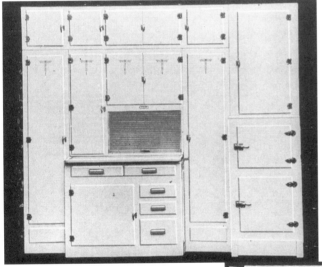

rated with Canadian-made furniture in the neo-classic style of the eighteenth-century English architect Robert Adam.[5]

The Canadian commissioner general in Paris, Philippe Roy, urged Ottawa to accept the invitation to the Paris exposition. 'The French Government seems to be very desirous that our country should take a part in their Exposition, which I believe is going to be well prepared and promise to be a success.' Roy had written to Tolmie, inviting him to come to Paris to meet French exposition officials, but had received no answer. He reminded Sir Joseph Pope, the under-secretary of state for external affairs, that the French government had contributed four million francs to 'The Canadian Train,' a trade- and immigration-boosting exhibition which had toured France the previous year. 'Please bring the Prime-Minister's attention to this matter,' he pleaded. But W.J. Egan, the deputy minister of immigration and colonization, announced shortly thereafter, on 14 April 1924, that 'consideration has been given to the question of Canada's participation in the International Exhibition ... to be held in Paris next year' and 'it has been decided not to take any action in this direction.'[6]

The furnishings purchased at the Paris exposition by the T. Eaton Company and other Canadian retailers were bought from French decorative-arts galleries, which built their own luxurious pavilions for the event. These Parisian galleries and department stores commissioned original designs from European artists, architects, and craftspeople and were a well-spring of inspiration for international buyers. While much of the furniture was severely elegant, some of it was decidedly eccentric, and one journalist claimed that 'no Canadian or American buyer came back from the Exposition without at least one purchase of which he might be a little bit terrified.'[7]

European exhibitors at the 1925 Paris exposition would have faced no threat from the Canadians, who manufactured office furniture, English and French 'period' furniture, or North American 'colonial' styles. But the exposition would have been an excellent opportunity to present North American furnishings in the absence of the Americans, and a selection of the best work from Canada should have constituted a reasonable display. There was certainly a sufficient number of manufacturers to choose from. James Acton, in his *Book of Canadian Furniture*, published in Toronto in 1923, lists 137 furniture manufacturers in Canada, with 108 of these in Ontario, 19 in Quebec, 4 in British Columbia, 2 in Manitoba, and 4 in Nova Scotia.[8] Their factories produced chairs, tables, beds, desks, cabinets, and chests of drawers in wood, metal, and reed (cane).[9]

The furniture made by these manufacturers was generally quite stolid, the only lightweight wooden furniture available being the bentwood seating and tables designed by Michael Thonet in the mid-nineteenth century, which was exported to Canada from Thonet Brothers' factories in Europe. These designs were subsequently produced by Canadian manufacturers when trade with Austria and Germany was halted by the First World War (fig.10). Bentwood furniture was not advertised to the general public, however, only to proprietors and managers of hotels, restaurants, and other commercial establishments (figs.11 and 12). One

Fig. 10 Café chair: bent solid wood, hand-woven cane (also made with embossed wood seat), mahogany or golden oak finish. Made in Canada. Distributed by McLaughlin Soda Fountain Company, Toronto, *ca* 1920. Probably made by the Owen Sound Chair Company, Owen Sound, Ontario (McLaughlin Soda Fountain Company catalogue, Metropolitan Toronto Reference Library, Special Collections)

Fig. 11 Café with bentwood chairs, Vancouver, *ca* 1920 (City of Vancouver Archives/99-77)

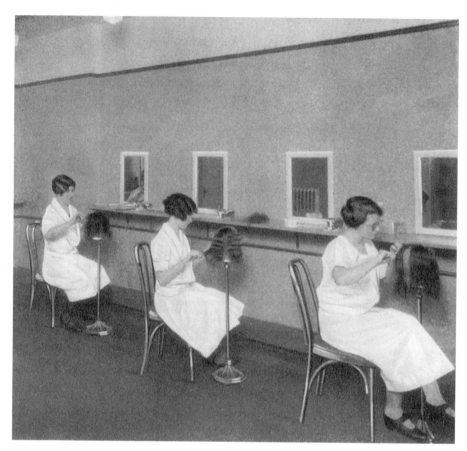

Fig. 12 The Danforth School of Beauty Culture, Toronto, with painted bentwood chairs. Advertisement showing student 'beauty culture operators' practising on wigs, in *Canadian Homes and Gardens* (November 1926)

European bentwood manufacturer, the influential German firm of Jacob and Joseph Kohn and Mundus, opened a contract showroom in downtown Toronto and advertised in the *The Canadian Hotel Review* in 1928: 'For business men's lunch, for banquet hall, and for the most fashionable dining room – there is always a suitable bentwood chair.'[10]

The stark contrast between the simple European café chairs and heavy Canadian household furnishings made the arrival of the new look from Europe seem somewhat overdue. Merchandise from France was eagerly promoted (fig. 13), and many retailers and manufacturers copied the most popular imports, producing an impressive quantity of furniture, light fixtures, wall-coverings, and every imaginable accessory. Retailers also sold the new 'French' designs from manufacturers in Grand Rapids, Michigan, the heart of the American wood-furniture industry.

In 1921, *The Grand Rapids Furniture Record*, an authoritative trade journal, had featured a story on a new store opened by the Adams Furniture Company on Yonge Street, in Toronto. Consisting of eight departments on six floors, plus a mezzanine, the store occupied a total of 85,000 square feet. The *Grand Rapids* staff reporter declared that 'the store is decorated so artistically that but for the furniture on display it might be mistaken for a bank.'[11] Founded in 1881 as a branch of the C.F. Adams Furniture Company, of Erie, Pennsylvania, the Toronto business had been bought in 1896 by its manager, Charles C. Coryell, with other Canadian stockholders. His son, Robert Coryell, was president of the company at the time of the opening of the Yonge Street store, which was the largest furnishings store in Canada. Full-time advertising and display managers were retained, the firm being noted for its 'artistic publicity,' which must have been effective as it was estimated by the company that they had 'an instalment account in every sixth home in Toronto.'

This proliferation of new furniture, fabrics, and decorative objects during the 1920s shifted the focus from modern efficiency in kitchens and bathrooms to modern glamour in living rooms, dining rooms, and bedrooms. The sequence of this domestic transformation in wealthier homes was usually from the private parts of the house to the public, with the principal sitting and dining rooms often retaining their Queen Anne– or Jacobean-reproduction splendour long after other rooms had been thoroughly revamped.

The T. Eaton Company and its principal rival, the Robert Simpson Company, advertised interior-decorating services intended to assist customers in their purchases at the store and to facilitate the subsequent installation of purchased goods. These services were doubtless a valued aid for customers overwhelmed by the profusion of new products, and represented a significant employment opportunity for young local designers.

Fig. 13 Furniture and fabric from France, the Robert Simpson Company (*Canadian Homes and Gardens*, April 1926)

Fig. 14 Chair by the Toronto Rattan Company (*Canadian Homes and Gardens*, April 1929)

Fig. 15 Illustration from advertisement for rattan and cane furniture by Imperial Rattan Company, Stratford, Ontario, in *Canadian Homes and Gardens* (November 1925)

Fig. 16 Cane and rattan armchair made by the Imperial Rattan Company, Stratford, Ontario, *ca* 1928 (Photo: Jeremy Jones, Toronto, 1992)

Model rooms and homes in the department stores attracted large, enthusiastic crowds. The interest was not entirely attributable to the intrigue of modernism, however, as very large crowds (70,000 visitors in two weeks) had turned out to see Simpson's 'Budget Bungalow' in Toronto in 1924, which was furnished in a mishmash of period styles.[12] But there was a real sense of high-toned adventure in the creation of these model rooms, and in published updates on modern design such as that written by Adele Gianelli in the new national magazine *Canadian Homes and Gardens*:

> The grotesque and amusing experiments in art and decoration that electrified Europe during the post-war period are seen now to have been the first rough wrench from the old, sacrosanct traditions ... From these first experiments there has been a steady progression toward a style that, unborrowed and underived, would express, through the media of woods, metals, and fabrics, the new spirit animating our literature, our music, our architecture, our art.[13]

Early Canadian forays into modernistic home decoration were often concealed within the long-standing fashion of orientalism, which had popularized the use of wallpapers, borders, rugs, prints, ceramics, and textiles whose decorative patterns were based on traditional designs from China, Japan, India, and Persia (plate 2). The drawing rooms of the aesthetically adventurous across the country were slowly transformed during the 1920s by these richly patterned fabrics, accessories, and cane furniture (figs. 14–16), all of which helped to set the scene for the exotic work from Paris. The Canweld Forge, in Montreal, advertised mirrors, in sumptuous frames, to 'reflect the dusky bloom of Oriental weave.' Japanese lanterns were purchased for city gardens, and the history and theory of Japanese painting and flower-arranging were presented in women's magazines. Art-Reed Furniture, made by the Toronto Rattan Company, was described as 'arrestingly lovely in its Chinese jade finish' (figs. 17 and 18). In 1927, a reception room in Rideau Hall, the governor general's residence in Ottawa, was redecorated as a 'Chinese Gallery' to accommodate a large collection of oriental decorative arts.[14] Cane furniture in less-exalted living rooms and sun rooms was accompanied by ginger-jar lamps and exotic plants, providing an appropriate setting for the judicious use of elaborate modernistic fabrics (fig. 19). The preference for patterns was captured by a 1927 advertisement for Maximur Wallpapers, of Toronto, which featured a quotation from 'the most famous decorator on this continent,' the American Elsie de Wolfe. 'Plain walls,' de Wolfe proclaimed, 'are the refuge of the artistically destitute' (fig. 20).

Even so, the new geometric patterns and shapes from the Paris exposition caused a stir. Early exhibitions of modernistic home settings at Eaton's (figs. 21–3) and Simpson's stores included bold fabrics and wallpapers that were disconcerting for many shoppers because they were not delicately pretty in the conventional manner of the popular paisleys and Chinese florals. Dramatic upholstery and drapery fabrics purchased at the 1926 Paris exposition by Louis Mulligan, a

Fig. 18 Another view of the Toronto Rattan Company show-room (*Canadian Homes and Gardens*, November 1928)

Fig. 19 Illustration from advertisement for the T. Eaton
Company. Caption: 'Summer Days – Very pleasant they can
be on a verandah, with cool reed furniture, gay chintz, col-
orful rugs and the picturesque setting that modernity pro-
vides for the semi-outdoor life' (*Canadian Homes and
Gardens*, July 1927)

Fig. 20 'Modernism in Wallpapers of Canadian Manufacture' (*Canadian Hotel Review*, 1929)

Fig. 21 Living-room setting, the
T. Eaton Company, Toronto (*Canadian
Homes and Gardens*, June 1928)

Fig. 22 Bedroom setting, the T. Eaton
Company, Toronto (*Canadian Homes
and Gardens*, June 1928)

Modern Furniture in Canada

Fig. 23 Sitting room with alcove seating, the T. Eaton Company, Toronto (*Canadian Homes and Gardens*, November 1928)

Montreal decorative-arts dealer, were cautiously recommended as 'bizarre but effective.'[15] The fashion for orientalism in Canada had not progressed so far as it had in England – people here did not recline on floor cushions at fashionable parties, as they did in Chelsea – and so the appearance of very low seating, often without legs, was also unsettling. As Alice Cooper observed in *Canadian Homes and Gardens*: 'The modern maiden shows most of her legs, but modern furniture tries to dispense with them.'[16]

Attention was often called to the difference between English and French furnishings. The French were admired for their technical virtuosity and love of luxury, and it was this image of French glamour that was successfully exploited by manufacturers and department stores (fig. 24). Simple decorative veneer-work, often using triangles and fan shapes, was meant to convey the effect of intricate inlay and marquetry. French names were obligatory. The Knechtel Furniture Company, in Hanover, Ontario, advertised their furniture – to English-speaking customers – as 'Mobilier à la mode de demain' or as 'Les Dernieres Creations … pour les ultra chic' (fig. 25). Office Specialty, an English manufacturer with sales offices throughout Canada, advertised 'L'Art Moderne' Matched Office Suites (in stainless steel), while Eaton's first line of modern American wood furniture was called 'Dynamique Creations.'

But French design was also associated with decadent frivolity or, even worse, the radical European avant-garde. More modest furniture from British craftsmen and manufacturers, on the other hand, was praised for its socially conscious, sensible approach to design. Adele Gianelli explained the critical difference: 'The furniture and colour schemes developed by modern French and German decorators may sometimes appear incoherent to the conservative Anglo-Saxon, but the work of the young British artists … has a marked simplicity and dignity. This English furniture is no wanton setting-up of *outré* shapes.'[17]

The new furniture posed a significant problem for families with valued collections of older furnishings who also wanted to be up-to-date:

> The possibilities of modernistic furniture in combination with pieces patterned after the historic periods are the subject of much consideration at the present time. The extreme modernist will brook no compromise with the past; he is passionately twentieth-century from the cellar to the garret. The average person, however, is less revolutionary; though he may be interested in the new movement, he is hardly prepared to scrap a houseful of furnishings gathered over a period of years and representing expenditure of time and money.[18]

This was the real challenge for manufacturers and retailers – to persuade reluctant families to replace older furnishings with new styles (figs. 26–9). The department stores and home-furnishing shops built across the country in the 1920s and 1930s were confidently but conservatively modern, designed to inspire and reassure. The displays at Eaton's and Simpson's were carefully composed. In 1927, for example, Eaton's Queen Street store in Toronto commissioned wrought-iron display stands for hats and scarves that were extravagant creations, inspired by shapes of

Fig. 24 Display of French furnishings at the Robert Simpson Company, Toronto (*Canadian Homes and Gardens*, November 1928)

Fig. 25 Advertisement for Knechtel Furniture Company, Limited, Hanover, Ontario, in *Canadian Homes and Gardens* (March 1929)

Fig. 26 Living room of Captain W. Roy Maxwell, Clarendon Apartments, Toronto, with French furniture, walls covered with blue grass-cloth, and floor in taupe broadloom. Decorated by Guy Mitchell of the Robert Simpson Company (*Canadian Homes and Gardens*, November 1928)

Fig. 27 Illustration from advertisement for hardwood floors. Caption: 'Furniture styles are changing' (*Canadian Homes and Gardens*, October 1928)

birds and foliage.[19] The three-storey shop designed for the Thornton Smith Company by John M. Lyle was awarded a Medal of Honour at the 1926 exhibition of the Ontario Association of Architects, and the stores themselves, as well as the furnishings they sold, were widely publicized. Some observers quickly proclaimed the victory of the new order: 'The modern influence in decorative art is now a definite and accepted fact. So intently, so persistently has it been brought to our attention that it has passed from what seemed to be a passing whim to be indulged in by a daring few, to a well-established expression of our day.'[20]

Eaton's hired a young French architect, René Cera, to design furniture and room settings for their stores and for clients' homes. 'I come to bring you the motives that are at work among the designers of Europe,' he announced to the press upon his arrival.[21] Cera's perception of the aesthetic status of Canadian design and manufacturing was realistic, and conveniently sales-oriented: 'You have no past, but you have a future.'

The most elaborate of Cera's installations was 'The House of Today,' first shown in 1929 at the Eaton's store in Calgary, Alberta (figs. 30 and 31). This model home was designed using simple geometric forms, in the spirit of Parisian architect Robert Mallet-Stevens. However, as its principal purpose was to display merchandise, it was crammed full with furnishings and accessories, and every surface was artfully sprinkled with items from other Eaton's departments: books, magazines, clothing, vases, tableware, even preserves. The design throughout was relentlessly modern, in an eclectic variety of fashionable styles, while the colouring was relatively restrained, using light green, pale beige, lemon yellow, pale pink, and taupe.

Mary-Etta Macpherson, the first regular writer on modern furniture and decoration for *Canadian Homes and Gardens*, reported on the Eaton's Calgary experiment: 'Picture a house of gray-white stucco; ... try to imagine an entire interior of sweeping and dramatic force, where walls are plain and lights glow from concealed troughs or niches, where only the furniture and accessories of the 20th Century have been given a place, and where the arts of this age are welcomed ... and you will have some inkling of *la maison d'aujourd'hui*.'[22] Macpherson was confident that 'The House of Today' would generate 'tremendous interest and stimulus' among those for whom the romantic past had little personal appeal. She discussed the ensemble (the 'assembling of all details to make a perfect unit') and was particularly impressed in this regard by the careful orchestration of the lighting – table lamps, glass and nickel-plated wall and ceiling fixtures, frosted strips of glass around ceilings, and glass cupboards with silvered backs and concealed interior lights. She also applauded the breakfast nook, which she saw as an answer to the modern demands for speed and simplicity, 'even in eating.' 'The House of Today' was, for Macpherson, 'the first concrete example of Canadian moderne.'

In Montreal, traditionally inspired *moderne* wooden furnishings lent an urbane air to redecorated rooms (fig. 32) and important new homes (fig. 33). A glamorous new department, l'Intérieur Moderne, was opened in Eaton's Montreal store in 1928. Under the direction of Jeannette Meunier, a young graduate of l'École des

Fig. 28 Living-room setting at the first Exposition of Art Moderne, the T. Eaton Company, Toronto (*Canadian Homes and Gardens*, November 1928)

Fig. 29 Illustration from advertisement for 'Art Moderne ... Low Furniture' showing bedroom decorated by the T. Eaton Company Interior Decoration Bureau (*Canadian Homes and Gardens*, October 1928)

Fig. 30 Living room in 'The House of Today,' the T. Eaton Company, Calgary, 1929. Designed by René Cera (Provincial Archives of Ontario/AO288)

Fig. 31 Bedroom in 'The House of Today,' the T. Eaton Company, Calgary. Designed by René Cera (*Canadian Homes and Gardens*, June 1929)

Beaux Arts, this *salon* displayed local and imported furnishings, mixing the more severe of the American products from Grand Rapids with a wide variety of other types of furniture and accessories, including expensive European wallpapers and upholstery fabrics (fig. 34).

Modern retail displays, however, were the exception to the rule. Department stores, decorative-arts shops, and home-decorating magazines throughout the country championed the new, but not at the expense of the old. Manufacturers and retailers strived to cater to all tastes, sometimes within the confines of one line of furniture. The Henry Morgan and Company department store in Montreal, for example, advertised a dining set in 1925 that was described as 'a strictly modern suite that retains much of the Early Colonial spirit. There are traces of Queen Anne and a touch of Italian heritage.'[23]

Mary-Etta Macpherson's articles in *Canadian Homes and Gardens* showed no such confusion. She was devoted to the domestic delights of modern design, although she definitely did not approve of avant-garde European designers, whom she criticized for showing 'as much refinement as a saxophone solo' and whom she curtly and irretrievably dismissed as being 'in error.' She also declared herself weary of the word 'modernistic' and of people 'playing modernist, shocking the world.' But Macpherson discussed new styles clearly and simply, and made practical suggestions for their implementation. She could write persuasively of such mundane details as 'the bright touch of colored enamels,' and addressed herself to middle-class as well as upper-class readers, with articles such as 'Cheerful Modernism for the Small House' (fig. 35). Her tone was sensible and upbeat, endorsing modern decoration as a tangible expression of *joie de vivre*.[24]

The modish vocabulary of the fashion pages had been appropriated by reporters and advertisers to describe the new furnishings. Macpherson drew a direct, physical connection between trends in fashion design and furniture design: 'The uncorseted debutante of 1929 has a dozen different ways of sitting in a chair and she insists that the chair be comfortable regardless of the posture.' Later, a full-page colour advertisement by Snyder's, a furniture manufacturer in Waterloo, showed a young woman *lounging* provocatively in a modern club chair while an elderly woman seated opposite declares: 'It was not the thing to do when I was a girl' (plate 4).

Manufacturers held open houses at least once every year. About 3,000 'buyers from all over the United States and Canada' attended the important semi-annual shows in Grand Rapids, held in January and June.[25] In Kitchener, Ontario, in January 1929, an impressive total of 70 furniture and fabric companies opened their factories to the trade and to the public. Macpherson, who spent three days viewing the Kitchener displays, commended the 'soft, melting color schemes' and the 'fine calmness' of the new interiors. She observed the influence of *art moderne* everywhere and 'found modernism in sufficiently varying degrees to suit every need and every purse.' There was also an abundance of 'modernistic fabrics ... adapted to conservative forms,' and a new material, rayon, which was 'revolutionizing' upholstery. The future looked bright. Manufacturers were showing a sincere desire and a readiness to

Fig. 32 Basement entertainment room in Westmount, Quebec, with satin-upholstered seating and walls covered in Japanese paper. Decorated by the T. Eaton Company, Montreal (*Canadian Homes and Gardens*, June 1929)

Fig. 33 Library in the residence of architect Ernest Cormier, Montreal. Designed by Ernest Cormier (*Royal Architectural Institute of Canada Journal*, July 1932)

Fig. 34 Setting for a man's study in *l'Intérieur Moderne*, the T. Eaton Company, Montreal. Desk/side chair made by the Michigan Chair Company, Grand Rapids (*Canadian Homes and Gardens*, February 1929)

serve the changing needs of the Canadian people, according to Macpherson, and one could look forward to a time when Canada would have its own distinctive style and would not have to rely upon importations from Europe and the United States.[26]

In a feature article published the following month, titled 'The New Trends in Canadian Furniture,' Macpherson argued that 'the vogue for the essentially modern' was a significant opportunity for Canadian furniture manufacturers.

> Furniture has become news. In the last five or six years it has undergone a swift and dramatic metamorphosis; from a comparatively humble position in the general scheme of things, from being a commodity, sometimes beautiful, always necessary, furniture has advanced to a place of major importance. It is important as a subject [and] ... as a symbol.
>
> Until perhaps a year ago, we in Canada were forced to rely on European centres for news of developments in the design and production of ... modern furniture. Within the past twelve months that situation has changed. The furniture industry ... has not been slow to feel the impact of the new movement, and even the first tentative efforts of our Canadian manufacturers along this line possess qualities which should win attention and encouragement for their makers.[27]

In the spring of that year, a dining suite by Emile-Jacques Ruhlmann was imported from France by Eaton's and exhibited at the Art Gallery of Toronto (now the Art Gallery of Ontario). The setting (figs. 36 and 37) comprised a Macassar ebony dining table, chairs, side table, vitrine, and buffet, all with metal details, and chairs upholstered in cherry-coloured leather. There was also a large rug with a geometric design in beige, grey, mulberry, coral, and Delft blue, and a striking minimalist glass-and-metal hanging lamp. The arrangement was described in *Canadian Homes and Gardens* as an important ensemble of 'subdued brilliance.' This enlightened tribute to the Parisian master of refined luxury and exquisite craftsmanship was somewhat marred by a subsequent Eaton's advertisement featuring the sale of the pieces from the gallery installation, and announcing that any of the designs could be reproduced or 'adapted.'

The Royal York Hotel opened in Toronto in the summer of 1929. The tallest building in the British Empire, it was described by its owners – Canadian Pacific Railway – and by awed reporters as 'an architectural triumph.' Every guest room had a radio that could be tuned to an outside station as well as to broadcasts from the hotel's own ballroom and convention rooms. There was also a hotel 'communications system' (pneumatic tube); 'numerous smart shops'; a bank; recreation centres; an emergency hospital; a printing plant; workshops for upholsterers, silversmiths, and locksmiths; even provisional conduits for television ('if television does come about then the Royal York is prepared'). The hotel boasted 'more than 1000 rooms with bath.'

Fig. 35 Illustration from article titled 'Cheerful Modernism for the Small House.' Dining room decorated by the Robert Simpson Company. Walnut and mahogany furniture made by the North American Furniture Company, Owen Sound, Ontario (*Canadian Homes and Gardens*, February 1929)

Fig. 36 Dining room designed by Emile-Jacques Ruhlmann, Paris. Installation at the Art Gallery of Toronto, sponsored by the T. Eaton Company, 1929 (*Canadian Homes and Gardens*, April 1929)

Fig. 37 Another view of dining room by Ruhlmann, installed at the Art Gallery of Toronto (*Canadian Homes and Gardens*, April 1929)

Fig. 38 The Art Moderne Suite, the Royal York Hotel, Toronto, 1929 (Canadian Pacific Limited Archives/M 435)

One of them was modern (fig. 38). All the other guest rooms, as well as the hotel's lobby, dining rooms, and ballroom, were decorated in an 'international pageant of styles' by Kate Treleaven, private secretary to E.W. (later Sir Edward) Beatty, president of Canadian Pacific Railway. Miss Treleaven's personality, 'expressed in terms of interior decoration and furnishing', was reported to be known to the vast number of Canadians and world travellers who had visited Canadian Pacific hotels in Ottawa, Regina, Vancouver, Victoria, and Banff.[28] The unprecedented 'Art Moderne Suite' at the Royal York was decorated in a range of browns, from 'linen to tobacco,' and was described by *The Canadian Hotel Review* as charmingly original and essentially comfortable, but severely masculine.[29]

Canadian Pacific trains were stylishly comfortable, and the company's ocean liners, criss-crossing the Atlantic and the Pacific, were decorated with élan by British and European designers, promoting foreign sophistication as the primary reward of the voyage. Canadian Pacific hotels, however, promoted stolid Canadian conservatism, and Miss Treleaven's personality.

The stock-market crash of 1929 was not mentioned in *Canadian Homes and Gardens* or in its sister publication, the fashion and society magazine *Mayfair*. The readers of these monthly magazines apparently continued to buy fur coats, cars, and boats. They visited New York, decorated houses, and entertained equally fortunate friends. Younger hostesses, according to one advertiser, were absorbed by the thrill of discovery, finding new ways to delight guests (in this instance by using 'impressively correct damask').[30] While there were few, if any, references to the Depression by journalists and editors, some advertisers made carefully guarded allusions to the stricken economy. Snyder's described their armchairs as 'great big "cushy" things for harassed nervous systems,' and Moore-Bell Limited, of Stratford, Ontario, went out of their way to stress the financial advantages of a folding screen: 'In any one of its many new versions, the screen is perhaps the most important of the minor decorative transforming notes within the reach of any room and purse. For the room that lacks in colour, in character, in dignity, in height, in smartness or even in beauty of furniture, just the right screen may be the miracle needed.' These simple, hinged, wood-framed folding panels provided manageable portions of modern pattern and colour, and the possibility of subsequent updating of a room, for the cost of just a few yards of fabric.

The true state of the economy, and the extreme fragility of the consumer-goods market, was revealed by the virtual disappearance of advertising for new furniture designs during 1930 and 1931. The Great Depression reinforced the perennial caution of Canadian manufacturers, and throughout the 1930s less than 10 per cent of the editorial and advertising space devoted to home furnishings featured contemporary designs.[31]

Fig. 39 Interior Decoration class, Ontario College of Art, Toronto, 1934 (Ontario College of Art prospectus, 1935)

The Furniture
Professions

The growing interest in professional interior design, initiated in the 1920s by department stores and decorative-arts dealers, led to the establishment of new design courses at several art schools. The Ontario College of Art was the first to add interior decoration to its curriculum, in 1930, as a 'specialist' course in the Department of Design and Applied Art, under Gustave Hahn. The official announcement in the school prospectus pointed out that interior decoration had 'always been touched upon' at the college but that now it had 'been decided to concentrate more definitely on the subject' (fig. 39). First-year students shared a foundation course with other students in the department. In second year, they received instruction in the fundamentals of architecture and furniture design, as well as studying form and colour in the composition and decoration of a room. Third year featured historic styles and 'original modern designs.' Fourth year repeated this combination, allocating segments of terms to 'research, adaptation and invention.' The college calendar promised that these endeavours would be thorough and practical; that the work would be as professional as possible; and that the new courses, in combination with crafts and design studies, would prove of great value to the serious student.

In the same year, a new school, l'École du Meuble, was established in Montreal, offering a two-year cabinetry apprenticeship program, which was expanded in 1935 by a supplementary two-year course in interior decoration and applied art. Under the direction of Louis-Athanase David and Jean-Marie Gauvreau, the school adhered to French craft traditions, emphasizing woodworking skills. This was seen to be a positive nationalist strategy to provide skilled employment and regionally distinctive furniture for Montreal's rapidly growing population. The example of fine craftsmen using Québécois woods was also intended to promote lumber sales to local and foreign furniture manufacturers, architects, and interior decorators.

In 1929, after his return from decorative-arts studies at l'École Boulle in Paris, Gauvreau had published a small book titled *Nos intérieurs de demain* which was principally a tribute to his French teachers, illustrated with photographs of elegant Parisian interiors and exhibition displays, both modern and traditional.[1] Although the work shown and discussed in *Nos intérieurs de demain* was all from Paris (fig.40), Gauvreau described the book as an attempt to show Canadians what was happening 'in modern art around the world.' And though the tone of the book is extravagant in its homage to Parisian masters, American mass-production designers are criticized for copying the French work that Gauvreau recommends as a model for Quebec craftsmen. Gauvreau was dismayed by the popularity in Montreal of the new, mass-produced furniture from Grand Rapids. Design, for him, was a matter of artistic taste that could be expressed adequately only through fine craftsmanship based on the craftsman's 'thousand little secrets' of success. This was a worthy but limited range of interest for a self-proclaimed modernist and influential teacher.

Canada had no authoritative figures arguing for a new theoretical framework for design, no propagandists for industrial design and modern decorative arts outside the department stores and the popular magazines (fig. 41). Critical writing about architecture was confined to the *Journal of the Royal Architectural Institute of Canada*, a precisely designed and crisply printed monthly magazine that reviewed new buildings in Canada and elsewhere. The journal did not report, however, on projects by the European avant-garde, thereby sparing Canadian architects the discomfort of seeing work that was radically different from their own. Le Corbusier's Pavillon de l'Esprit Nouveau at the 1925 Paris exposition, for example, was not included in the journal's reports on that event. Significant new work could only be glimpsed in the magazine's occasional surveys of foreign buildings, in which the best work was often dismissed with a single line of derisory text. In 1930, the writer of one such article condemned an important new school by architect Willem Dudok in Hilversum, Holland, with the question: 'How could anything be sillier than the notched-out surfaces which involve all sorts of senseless cantilevering?'

The Toronto Chapter of the Royal Architectural Institute of Canada (RAIC) had responded to the widespread interest in the decorative arts by sponsoring

Fig. 40 Interior designed by Louis Sognot with furnishings by Primavera at the Exposition Internationale des Arts Décoratifs et Industriels Modernes, Paris 1925 (*Nos intérieurs de demain*, Montreal, 1929)

Fig. 41 Window display, the Robert Simpson Company, Toronto, 1931. Tubular-steel table and chair designed by Marcel Breuer, Germany, 1927, made by Thonet (Hudson's Bay Company Archives, Provincial Archives of Manitoba)

Fig. 42 Study decorated by 'The House of Today,' the T. Eaton Company, sponsored by the Junior League of Toronto (*Canadian Homes and Gardens*, June 1930)

Fig. 43 The Artists' Workshop studio, Montreal. Chair and chest of drawers in grey harewood, table in wrought aluminum (*Canadian Homes and Gardens*, June 1939)

Fig. 44 Master bedroom in country home built for the McMartin family at the Seigniory Club, Montebello, Quebec. Furniture designed by Gert Lamartine, the Artists' Workshop, Montreal (*Canadian Homes and Gardens*, August–September 1935)

and installing annual allied-arts exhibitions in The Grange at the Art Gallery of Toronto. The popular success of the first of these exhibitions in 1927 – the catalogues sold out by the sixth day – was attributed by the well-known architect John M. Lyle to the 'great diversity' and 'effective handling' of the exhibits.[2] Photographs of the exhibition, however, show that the only furnishings on display were imposing antiques and elaborate reproductions, and that the arrangements were uniformly awkward, with pieces lined up in rows against the walls.[3] An alternative strategy, the arrangement of *ensembles* to show rooms and furniture as used in real life, was common by this time in European and American exhibitions, as well as in retail displays in many countries, including Canada (fig. 42). But this effective way of presenting new furnishings to the public must have been unknown to members of the institute, whose journal did not publish photographs of furniture or interior architecture exhibitions.

The 1927 exhibition, the first of many annual RAIC shows at the gallery, would have justified the scathing public criticism that was finally unleashed after the fifth show, in 1931. E.H. Blake, a 'layman,' explained in an article for the journal that he found it curious that the exhibition presented so few examples of 'anything that might be described as the thorough modern manner.'

> In this respect I should think that this exhibition must be unique among contemporary exhibitions of a similar range and its barrenness in modern work must prompt some searching questions. Does it mean that we are denying the epoch of machinery in which we live, and producing worthless, insignificant buildings that not only fail to reflect, but actually attempt to disguise the civilization of our time? Does it mean that our architects, content with plagiarism, are burying their brains as well as their buildings under the accumulated rubbish of the past?[4]

An article in the journal in 1932, discussing styles 'suitable for Canadian domestic architecture,' argued that the conservatism of the architectural profession was imposed by the clients: 'The romantic versus formal, modern versus traditional. Having regard to the predilections of our clients, the traditionalists have much the better of the modernists. The traditional modernist is a compromise, and a selection of the best work of recent years shows that this is the prevailing tendency at the present time.'[5] The preference for traditional styles in houses and furnishings was encouraged by the reluctance of Canadian financial institutions to arrange mortgages for modern, flat-roofed houses, whose potential for snow accumulation was perceived as a serious risk. An architect writing in the journal went out of his way to excuse this national timidity. 'Modern is a rather confusing term,' he pleaded, 'and one cannot entirely blame the mortgagee for being a bit slow in accepting it.'[6] While the steeply pitched roofs and small windows of Canadian homes did not absolutely prevent expression of early twentieth-century modernist ideals in domestic architecture, they certainly limited their development. The cautious, conservative style of home decoration was thus reflected and reinforced by the traditional appearance of Canadian towns and neighbourhoods.

Fig. 45 Chair and table: painted wrought iron, woven cane, glass. Designed by Kenneth Noxon. Made by Metalsmiths, Toronto (*Canadian Homes and Gardens*, May 1938)

Fig. 46 Garden furniture: painted wrought iron, glass. Designed by Kenneth Noxon. Made by Metalsmiths, Toronto (*Canadian Homes and Gardens*, May 1938)

HAND MADE

Porch Railings
Interior Stair Rails
Gates —Grilles

Lanterns
Ceiling Fixtures
Wall Brackets
Floor Lamps
Table Lamps

Andirons   Curbs
Grates
Firescreens
Firetools
Hoods   Cranes

Door and Window
Hardware
Footscrapers
Weathervanes
Signs
Drapery Hardware

Chairs   Tables   Mirrors
Fernstands
Candlesticks

When writing for catalogue, please state type of work interested in.

METALSMITHS CO. LTD. 921 Yonge St. TORONTO

Fig. 47 Advertisement for Metalsmiths, Toronto, in *Canadian Homes and Gardens* (April 1938)

Fig. 48 Armchair, table, and magazine rack: painted wrought iron, glass, upholstery. Designed by Kenneth Noxon. Made by Metalsmiths, Toronto (*Canadian Homes and Gardens*, June–July 1935)

The lack of interest in modernism among senior architects and their establishment clients was a deterrent to the local production of original furniture designs. But younger interior decorators, craftspeople, and architects were keen to push their work in new directions. In 1933, five McGill University architecture graduates set up a small design company called 'The Iron Cat,' and the two principal partners, James Woollven and Harold Devitt, did a great deal of custom residential work in the subsequent decades. The Artists' Workshop, also in Montreal, was a co-operative studio and showroom set up by a group of woodworkers and metalsmiths, including Gert Lamartine, a furniture designer/maker (fig. 43). His upholstered seating often used fabrics by the Montreal weaver Karen Bulow, who was justly famous for her rugs and for her 'filmy curtains and fine, damask-like draperies.'[7] Cabinetry and seating from the Artists' Workshop and fabrics by Bulow were used in many new or redecorated Quebec residences, including an extravagant 'hunting lodge' country home built in 1935 for the McMartin family at the Seigniory Club in Montebello (fig. 44).

Kenneth Noxon, a graduate architect from the University of Toronto, had established a more ambitious fabrication company, Metalsmiths, in Toronto in the mid-1920s. Noxon manufactured his own designs for chairs, tables, plant-stands, fire-screens, fireplace equipment, light fixtures, weather-vanes, and hardware of all types (figs. 45–8). These practical, refined, and imaginative pieces in wrought iron, cane, and glass were often advertised by Eaton's and seen in numerous published homes and model rooms. In an address to the National Arts Club in New York, the Canadian artist Elizabeth Wyn Wood reported that Noxon had 'made upward of five thousand designs'[8] and had 'gathered to his forges eight or nine entire families of craftsmen.' Noxon operated his own retail shops, at various locations over the years, on Yonge Street, where his ever-evolving range of products could be purchased or ordered.

In 1930, Eaton's opened a new department store at College and Yonge streets, devoted exclusively to the sale of home furnishings. It featured the city's most elegant restaurant, The Round Room (fig. 49), and a spacious, streamlined auditorium (fig. 50). The main floor, designed by Réne Cera, included the Lamp Department, and the Elevator Arcade, with walnut and chromed-metal display tables and tall, illuminated marble urns. The *RAIC Journal* cautiously advised, in a 1935 report on the new store, that this type of modern work had been 'accepted … by the Canadian layman' in commercial buildings. There was apparently still some doubt as to its acceptability in other types of buildings. The glamorous restaurant in the Eaton's Montreal store had, indeed, been the first modern interior published in the journal, in 1931 (figs. 51 and 52).

By the mid-1930s, Canadians could see modern furnishings being used in progressive commercial establishments, including stylish local branches of the international fashion and beauty business (figs. 53 and 54). They could also examine new types of merchandise offered for sale in local shops and stores. The majority of these products were made in Canada, sometimes in the department stores' own workshops. Most of the remainder was imported from the United States, with the addition of some unusual pieces from Europe (figs. 55 and 56).

Modern Furniture in Canada

Fig. 49 Restaurant, the T. Eaton Company, College Street, Toronto, 1935. Designed by Ross and Macdonald, Architects (Provincial Archives of Ontario/AO297)

Fig. 50 Auditorium, the T. Eaton Company, College Street, Toronto, *ca* 1935 (Provincial Archives of Ontario/AO287)

Fig. 51 Alcove in foyer of restaurant, the T. Eaton Company, Montreal. Ross and Macdonald, Architects; Jacques Corin, Associate Architect (*Royal Architectural Institute of Canada Journal*, May 1931)

Modern Furniture in Canada

Fig. 52 Restaurant, the T. Eaton Company, Montreal (*Royal Architectural Institute of Canada Journal*, May 1931)

Displays were spacious and elegant, and model-room installations were often remarkable for the clarity and severity of their assemblage (figs. 57 and 58). Professional decorators were able to help their more affluent clients in making judicious selections from pieces in the store, and in commissioning original designs from local craftspeople. The more adventurous decorators encouraged their clients to experiment with new types of *moderne* environments. These often involved mirrors – mirrored mantelpieces, wall niches lined with mirrors, or whole walls covered with mirrored panels – and were relatively simple strategies for transformation (fig. 59). 'The bathroom so treated would become one of those modern shrines of luxury that every woman yearns for.'[9]

The summers of the 1930s brought a profusion of modern garden and sun-room furniture in wood, rattan, wrought iron, tubular metal, and perforated sheet-metal. Their light, minimal shapes were easily absorbed into gardens and terraces (figs. 60–2) and informal areas inside the home. The Eaton's Interior Decorating Bureau advised that 'the contemporary style is ideal' for breakfast rooms, morning rooms, summer sitting rooms, and verandahs. Many types of modern chairs and tables were ambiguous as to their intended setting and were equally appropriate indoors or out (figs. 63 and 64).

The first cantilever chairs made in Canada were inexpensive adaptations of the MR20 armchair designed by German architect Mies van der Rohe (figs. 65 and 66). Those produced by the Standard Tube Company, a hospital-equipment manufacturer in Woodstock, Ontario, were covered 'in bright colours and gay materials.' The alarming new structure was introduced gently: 'If you have recently strolled into the smart salons that line New York's most fashionable thoroughfare, you will recall those different looking chairs you saw.'[10] Standard Tube later made, or imported, another German cantilever chair, the Desta SS34, designed by architect Erich Mendelsohn (fig. 67). Many of the furniture makers in southern Ontario were of German descent, and those using industrial methods of production would have been familiar with the first mass-produced, bent-tubular-steel furniture, designed by Marcel Breuer at the Bauhaus, Dessau, Germany, in 1925.

Changing social life affected the style and composition of rooms. Wealthy families installed impressively modern breakfast rooms (fig. 68) and dining rooms (fig. 69), although some of the latter were less than successful experiments (fig. 70). Living rooms were rearranged to accommodate the square table and four chairs needed for playing bridge (fig. 71). Bedrooms were lavished with extravagant details such as etched-glass doors, lacquered beds, and painted murals (fig. 72). Formal tables and upholstered seating, appropriate for many of the new rooms, were made by Snyder's in Waterloo, probably the largest furniture manufacturer in the country, and certainly one of the few Canadian companies whose products were nationally advertised and distributed (fig. 73).[11] A 1932 Snyder's advertisement for one of its colonial lines showed 'A Room that Can Be Created Anywhere in The Dominion.'

Fig. 53 Le Salon de Beauté, Morgan's, Montreal. Designed by Omer Parent *(Technique* 10/9, 1935)

Fig. 54 Helena Rubenstein Beauty Salon, Bloor Street West, Toronto (*Mayfair*, March 1930)

Fig. 55 Chair sold by the Robert Simpson Company (*Canadian Homes and Gardens*, June–July 1934)

Fig. 56 Chair designed by R.C. Coquery, France. Manufactured by Thonet (B251). Sold in Canada by the Robert Simpson Company (*Canadian Homes and Gardens*, June–July 1934)

Fig. 57 Cantilever lounge chair, three-seater swing sofa, armchair, and occasional tables: chrome-plated and enamelled flat steel, wood, upholstery. Made by the Dominion Chain Company, Niagara Falls, Ontario, and Niagara Falls, New York. Display at Eaton's, College Street, Toronto (*Canadian Homes and Gardens*, June–July 1934)

Fig. 58 Display of steel furniture at T. Eaton Company, Toronto (*Canadian Homes and Gardens*, July 1931)

Fig. 59 Drawing from the T. Eaton Company Interior Decoration Bureau, Toronto, showing living room with mirrored mantelpiece and indirect lighting (*Canadian Homes and Gardens*, March 1933)

Fig. 60 Garden in the Carse residence, Burlington, Ontario. Designed by Sheridan Nurseries (*Canadian Homes and Gardens*, December 1930)

Fig. 61 Backyard on Poplar Plains Road, Toronto, with tilting canopy on wheels, in metal and canvas, advertised by Eaton's (*Canadian Homes and Gardens*, July 1933)

Fig. 62 Armchair made by Imperial Rattan Company, Stratford, Ontario (*Canadian Homes and Gardens*, June 1932)

Fig. 63 Garden chair with canopy and table, in cane, rattan, canvas. Made by the Toronto Rattan Company (*Canadian Homes and Gardens*, June 1932)

Fig. 64 Cane and rattan furniture, venetian blinds, rug, and accessories, on display at T. Eaton Company, College Street, Toronto (advertisement in *Canadian Homes and Gardens*, June 1933)

Fig. 65 Display in T. Eaton Company, College Street, Toronto. Tubular-steel and laminated-wood table designed by Marcel Breuer, Germany, 1925–6. Tubular-steel armchair designed by Ludwig Mies van der Rohe, Germany, 1927. Both made by Thonet (*Canadian Homes and Gardens*, June 1933)

Fig. 66 Living room decorated by the T. Eaton Company, with steel-tube adaptation of Mies van der Rohe chair (*Canadian Homes and Gardens*, July 1930)

Fig. 67 Armchair: chrome-plated steel tube, wood, leather. Made, or imported, by the Standard Tube Company, Woodstock, Ontario (Photo: William Deacon 1985)

Fig. 68 Breakfast room in the home of Colonel W.E. Phillips, Oshawa, Ontario, decorated by the T. Eaton Company Interior Decorating Bureau (*Canadian Homes and Gardens*, May 1932)

Fig. 69 Dining room, mural painted by Charles Comfort (*Canadian Homes and Gardens*, January–February 1934)

Fig. 70 Dining room in the home of Othon Goetz, Rosedale, Toronto. Designed by 'a French artist,' unnamed, who 'employed the triangle as the dominant note throughout.' Furniture in bird's-eye maple, lacquered pale grey with black trim (*Canadian Homes and Gardens*, October–November 1934)

Fig. 71 Breakfast-room setting displayed at the Canadian National Exhibition, Toronto. Designed by Guy Mitchell of the Robert Simpson Company (*Canadian Homes and Gardens*, September 1938)

In November 1933, ten Toronto designers established the Society of Interior Decorators of Ontario. The charter members included Guy Mitchell, of the Robert Simpson Company; Robert Irvine, of the Thornton Smith Company (fig. 74); Archibald Chisholm and S.H. Maw, of Eaton's (fig. 75); Anne Harris, who had a shop on Charles Street East, in Toronto; John Ridpath, the retailer (fig. 76); and Freda James, at that time working for Ridpath's but later to open her own business on fashionable Grenville Street (fig. 77). By 1935 the group also included Laurence Barraud, Augusta Fleming, and R. Malcolm Slimon.[12] According to a November 1933 advertisement in *Canadian Homes and Gardens*, the society aimed to place interior decorating on 'a professional plane' and to advance the appreciation of 'good decorating.' The Interior Decorators Society of Quebec was founded in the same year by a similar group of decorative-arts gallery proprietors and department-store buyers. They recruited most of their membership from the graduates of the Interior Decoration department at l'École du Meuble. Both provincial associations regularly advertised their services in magazines, urging the Canadian public to 'consult a decorator.'

The apartment that Guy Mitchell designed in 1934 for Major A.C. Ryerson of Toronto was starkly modern (fig. 78). Black-painted walls, black carpet, black glass table-tops, and black-lacquered wood were used in counterpoint to mirrored glass, white leather, and generous quantities of chromed-steel tube. The previous year, Mitchell had converted a client's living room to add an alcove for bridge-playing and had decorated it with cherry-red drapes, a red and white saddle-stitched armchair, and white leather bridge chairs, on a shiny black and white linoleum floor. Mitchell's interiors demonstrated a cleverly subversive combination of formality and frivolity.

Thornton Smith, a Toronto retailer, described his firm's decoration staff as 'the inspirational force within our organization ... working under ideal conditions and with ideal co-operation from factory to finished product.' Subdued rooms emphasized the quality of the materials rather than their decorative effects (fig. 79). Simplicity and severity were the hallmarks of the new style, most obviously expressed in bare walls and monotone floor-coverings, sheer drapery, and white venetian blinds (figs. 80–9). Striped and plaid fabrics, often 'homespun,' in natural, earthy colours, replaced the bright stylized florals and complex geometric block-patterns of the 1920s. A home in Forest Hill Village, Toronto, redecorated in 1936 for the Honourable J. Earl Lawson, a lawyer and member of Parliament, incorporated all the new ideas – mirrored wall and ceiling panels in the living room; venetian blinds; plaid drapes; linoleum floors; and one predominant colour, oyster white, used throughout (fig. 90).

While private clients welcomed the services of interior decorators, Canadian furniture manufacturers found the concept of hiring professional designers a difficult one to grasp. Design development for them was a low-profile, in-house activity involving the proprietor, the factory manager, the woodwork and upholstery foremen, and the sales department. Final decisions were often made by sales managers, who met the store buyers regularly and were most keenly aware of competitors' products.

Fig. 72 Bedroom of Miss Mary O'Connor, in the home of Mr and Mrs Frank O'Connor, Toronto. Decorated in grey, orange, black, and silver (*Canadian Homes and Gardens*, April 1933)

Fig. 73 Drawing of living room by designer Whitney Dill of the Decoration Service, the Robert Simpson Company. Furniture by Snyder's (*Canadian Homes and Gardens*, April 1935)

Fig. 74 Basement entertainment room designed by K.M. Irvine and R.W. Irvine, Thornton Smith Company, Toronto. English hooked rug designed by Derek Patmore (*Canadian Homes and Gardens*, June 1937)

Fig. 75 Bedroom, the Little Display of Contemporary Furnishings, T. Eaton Company, College Street, Toronto, decorated in lemon-yellow, chartreuse, ivory, orange, and black. Furniture in elm burl, with ivory lacquer, made in the Eaton's cabinet shop. Photo caption: 'Furnishing in the Mode 1933' (Advertisement, *Canadian Homes and Gardens*, September 1933)

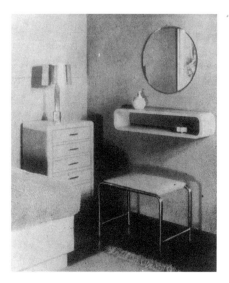

Fig. 76 Bedroom display in Ridpath's Limited, Toronto, mid-1930s. Bed and stool covered in leather (Advertisement, *Canadian Homes and Gardens*, January–February 1935)

Fig. 77 Living room in the redecorated residence of Alan Stephen, Headmaster of the Preparatory School, Upper Canada College, Toronto. Decorated by Freda James in green, blue, and grey, with linen-upholstered maple furniture, and mirrored panel above fireplace (*Canadian Homes and Gardens*, March 1935)

Fig. 78 Dining room in the apartment of Major A.C. Ryerson, Avenue Road, Toronto. Designed by Guy Mitchell of the Decoration Service, the Robert Simpson Company, in black and white, with mirrored glass, black glass, chrome-plated steel, white leather (*Canadian Homes and Gardens*, March 1934)

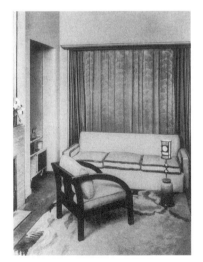

Fig. 79 Living room in peach, ivory, and beige, designed by René Cera, Eaton's, Toronto. Chair by Paul Frankl, New York, or copy (*Canadian Homes and Gardens*, September 1933)

As a result, new Canadian furniture continued to be based on the most popular work from other countries. The Andrew Malcolm Furniture Company, in Kincardine, and McLagan Furniture, in Stratford, both introduced lines of wooden furniture inspired by the work of Gilbert Rhode, design director for the Herman Miller Furniture Company, in Zeeland, Michigan (whose work in turn owed much to that of Marcel Breuer in Germany). However, advertisements for the Rhode-inspired Andrew Malcolm furniture stressed the 'true originality' of the designs. New products from both companies featured plain architectonic forms in veneered wood (figs. 91–4), with ornamentation limited to simple juxtapositions of dark and light woods, or of wood with metal and glass, and confined to the simplest geometric shapes.

An article titled 'Contemporary Decorative Art,' by Eleanor Stephens, in the April 1933 issue of *Canadian Homes and Gardens*, explained the difference between the early 1930s and 'the modernistic decade' of the 1920s, placing Canadian design in a larger historical context. Stephens noted the influence of Scottish architect and designer Charles Rennie Macintosh, and of Julius Meier-Graefe, a European decorative-arts dealer and critic.[13] She pointed out that geometry was vital to modern design, but that design was not simply a matter of geometry.

Curves had become 'flattened' in structures and ornamentation as the public had 'forsaken the exuberance of Victorian roses and peonies, for the elongated curves of lilies and tulips.' Fabrics and colours had become more subdued and refined as 'the contemporary style' aimed at achieving more 'restful surroundings.' Furniture was 'smaller in size, and scantier in quantity,' to better suit 'present-day habits and the sizes of our rooms.'

Stephens, in baffling refutation of her own historical references, claimed that 'comfort-loving England' was the source of all these changes. In Canada, she could see that the new decor was making converts daily. The movement was inevitable and would soon be 'universal' as one could no more resist the currents of our time than one could 'stay the flood of Niagara.'

Canadian manufacturers included decorating suggestions in their advertisements, such as these tips for the correct deployment of McLagan's new mahogany and maple bedroom furniture:

> Your complete furniture needs are represented here. With a little care in the
> matter of background and fabrics a distinguished room may be created. Pale
> lime green walls, painted or papered, curtains of a modern rough cotton
> plaid, in green or brown, a brown carpet and a lime green velveteen spread,
> and perhaps a touch of coral or scarlet in the small accessories ... your room
> takes on an immediate vitality.[14]

Fig. 80 Boardroom of Litho Print, Toronto. Table and chairs in maple, chesterfield in brown and beige linen, floor in rust linoleum. Designed by Eaton's Interior Decorating Department (*Canadian Homes and Gardens*, May 1936)

Fig. 81 Reception room of Litho Print, Toronto (*Canadian Homes and Gardens*, May 1936)

Fig. 82 Office of W.R. Hanna, president of Litho Print, Toronto. Desk and chair in maple; lounge chair in brown and beige linen; floor in rust, grey, and ivory linoleum. Designed by Eaton's Interior Decorating Department (*Canadian Homes and Gardens*, May 1936)

Fig. 83 Sun room with steel-tube furniture. Decorated by the T. Eaton Company Interior Decoration Bureau, College Street, Toronto (Advertisement, *Canadian Homes and Gardens*, April 1934)

Fig. 84 Display of steel-tube furniture. Robert Simpson Company (Advertisement, *Canadian Homes and Gardens*, April 1934)

Fig. 85 Wood desk, chromed-steel chair, metal lamps, and 'homespun' fabrics from the T. Eaton Company, College Street, Toronto (*Canadian Homes and Gardens*, September 1932)

Fig. 86 Living room of home in Hamilton, Ontario, by Hutton and Souter, Architects. Interior design by Freda James (*Canadian Homes and Gardens*, January–February 1936)

Fig. 87 Another view of living room in Hamilton home. Interior design by Freda James (*Canadian Homes and Gardens*, January–February 1936)

Fig. 89 Ilustration in advertisement for Sunniweb sheer drapery fabric manufactured by Canadian Celanese Limited, Montreal. Drawing by André Belier (*Canadian Homes and Gardens*, October 1933)

Fig. 90 Living room in the redecorated home of J. Earl Lawson, King's Counsel and Member of Parliament, Forest Hill, Toronto. Designed by the Decoration Service, the Robert Simpson Company. Table at left by Metalsmiths (*Canadian Homes and Gardens*, March 1937)

Fig. 91 Chest of drawers with round mirror, solid mahogany and maple. Made by the McLagan Furniture Company, Stratford, Ontario (Advertisement, *Canadian Homes and Gardens*, February 1934)

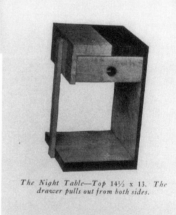

The Night Table—Top 14½ x 13. The drawer pulls out from both sides.

Fig. 92 Side table, solid mahogany and maple. Made by the McLagan Furniture Company, Stratford (Advertisement, *Canadian Homes and Gardens*, January–February 1934)

Fig. 93 Dressing table with tall rectangular mirror, solid mahogany and maple. Made by the McLagan Furniture Company, Stratford (Advertisement, *Canadian Homes and Gardens*, February 1934)

Fig. 94 High chest of drawers with small rectangular mirror (not attached), solid mahogany and maple. Made by the McLagan Furniture Company, Stratford (Advertisement, *Canadian Homes and Gardens*, February 1934)

Intriguing new furniture could be seen in foreign magazines and decorating books, which were widely available at bookstores in Canada. The authors of these books presented an array of professionally designed furnishings and professionally decorated rooms, in great detail, covering every possible consideration in the choice of colours and objects. The Studio series of periodicals and books, published in London and New York, gathered together impressive quantities of photographs from Britain, Europe, America, Scandinavia, and beyond, and were regarded and utilized as comprehensive, authoritative compendiums. A corner-view of a bedroom designed by Toronto architect Eric Arthur was published in a book titled *Furnishing the Small Home*, written by Margaret Merivale and published by The Studio Limited in 1938. Newly popularized ideas, such as streamlined club chairs, and animal-print drapes, spread quickly from one country to another (figs. 95 and 96), while eccentricities such as a fold-down armchair sold by Ridpath's (fig. 97) were quickly forgotten.

Design and decorating ideas from the United States were of two types. The 'machine' aesthetic of streamlining was evident in a wide variety of furnishings and equipment, from door handles to table lamps, to refrigerators, that featured smooth curves, round corners, and shiny finishes, with ornamentation limited to moulded edges, and thin, raised bands of chrome or enamel (plate 5). These stylized industrial motifs encouraged the use of new products such as glass bricks (figs. 98 and 99) and new materials such as Plexiglas (fig. 100) in residential and commercial interiors.

The other, predominant, American influence was an eclectic historicism popularized by American decorating magazines and subsequently adopted as the perennial decorating strategy of Canadian department stores. In this merchandising mêlée, a handful of historic styles of wood furniture were regularly updated with new colours and details to stimulate renewed purchasing demand among an established clientele.

The 1936 version of Snyder's well-established 'colonial' line, for example, was designed by the American industrial designer Russell Wright (plate 6). These living-room, bedroom, and dinette pieces, called 'Modern Maple,' were 'designed to express in the 20th century manner, the simplicity and frank construction of Colonial furniture' and, according to advertisements, were especially useful in small apartments. They featured 'Cushion Edge' on every piece – corners rounded to prevent chipping and to add 'beauty and form' to the furniture.

The new Toronto Stock Exchange, opened in 1937, was both modern and old-fashioned, by design. As conceived and executed by George and Moorhouse, Architects, with S.H. Maw, associate architect, the exchange presented a conservatively modern stone and glass façade to Bay Street, the financial hub of the country. The main trading floor (fig. 101), lobby, and other semi-public spaces were all dramatically streamlined, with high standards of finishing and detailing. The members' dining room was particularly effective, with the dark colours and strong curvilinear forms of the architecture echoed in the furniture (fig. 102). These rooms were intended to express the forward-looking, bustling nature of the new enterprise. The senior management offices and boardroom, on the other hand, were decorated in Queen Anne style, with fireplaces, wood panelling, and chandeliers, to emphasize the exchange's 'solid foundation.'[15]

Fig. 95 Living room in home of Mr and Mrs J.S. Duncan, Toronto. Designed by Eaton's Interior Decorating Bureau (*Canadian Homes and Gardens*, December 1937)

Fig. 96 Living room in apartment of C.S. Gunn, the Fort Garry Hotel, Winnipeg. Designed by Elsa Gordon and H.W. Cooper of Eaton's Interior Decorating Studio, Winnipeg, in brown and white with turquoise accents (*Canadian Homes and Gardens*, April 1937)

Fig. 97 Armchair, with fold-down seat cushion, 'designed especially for the comfort-loving man-of-the-house' (Advertisement for Ridpath's, Toronto, *Canadian Homes and Gardens*, December 1939)

Fig. 98 The Carlton Club, Montreal. Designed by Mathers and Haldenby, Architects (*Royal Architectural Institute of Canada Journal*, January 1937)

Fig. 99 Decorative-arts exhibition at the Art Gallery of Toronto, February 1937. Furnishings by Eaton's (Provincial Archives of Ontario/AD296)

The Park Plaza Hotel in Toronto, designed by architect Hugh G. Holman, was thoroughly modern. It featured unusual suites of furniture in its guest rooms, providing separate but adjacent sitting and sleeping areas. The furnishings were all modern and all made in Canada. They combined light woods with pale walls and plain fabrics (fig. 103), or chromed steel with dark walls and rich, patterned upholstery (fig. 104). In Vancouver, the newly redecorated Hotel Vancouver was glamorously *moderne*, with torchères, exotic woods, and rounded edges on every object and surface (fig. 105).

Similarly impressive furnishings were displayed in the Canada Pavilion at the 1937 Paris exposition, l'Exposition Internationale des Arts et Techniques dans la Vie Moderne. The Canada pavilion, although shaped like a grain silo and attached to one end of the United Kingdom pavilion, nevertheless marked an important advance in the presentation of the country's decorative arts (fig. 106). Canadian furniture was shown in a room setting of elegant proportions, decorated with dramatic wood panelling, geometrically patterned drapes and rugs, and concealed lighting. The same eminently successful setting, rearranged slightly and with one or two new pieces of furniture, was used again the next year at the British Industries Fair at Earl's Court (fig. 107).

A brochure was published by the Canadian Exhibition Commission at the end of 1937 and distributed to producers and manufacturers across the country. It explained the policies and practices of the commission and included useful tips for exhibitors.[16] At the New York World's Fair in 1939, a simple white Canada pavilion, with glass-block windows, demonstrated the traditional modernist style promoted in the pages of the *RAIC Journal*.[17]

The Royal Canadian Academy of Arts made a laudable but feeble attempt to interest the public in industrial design by organizing an exhibition, 'Canadian Industrial Arts,' at the Art Gallery of Toronto in 1938. Based on more adventurous exhibitions with similar titles in London and New York, 'Canadian Industrial Arts' was largely a display of traditional furnishings and tableware, as well as advertisements, packaging, and some appliances, most of which clearly lacked any original design.

An introductory essay in the exhibition catalogue awkwardly tried to claim some of the new design territory for the academy's members, who were painters and sculptors, by describing the exhibition as a survey of the field intended to 'stimulate the Canadian artist to design for manufacture' and support the 'fabrication of Canadian motifs.' The academy would 'feel repaid' if the exhibition 'quickened interest in an art quality in manufacture.' Such a response would support the academy's contention that 'those who are called artists' are more sensitive to beauty, and 'some are able to create it.'

Fig. 100 'Crystal Corner,' a display of Plexiglas products, the Robert Simpson Company, London, Ontario (*Canadian Homes and Gardens*, 1937)

Fig. 101 Trading floor, the Toronto Stock Exchange. Designed by George and Moorhouse, Architects; S.H. Maw, Associate Architect. Murals painted by Charles Comfort. Members' desks, white- and black-painted wood, with fold-down seats (*Royal Architectural Institute of Canada Journal*, April 1937)

Fig. 102 Members' dining room, the Toronto Stock Exchange (*Royal Architectural Institute of Canada Journal,* April 1937)

Model rooms at the 1940 Canadian National Exhibition in Toronto were described in the October 1940 issue of *Canadian Homes and Gardens* as 'Modern with a Purpose.' This headline was repeated six months later, in April 1941, to describe a new line of living-room, dining-room, and bedroom furniture made by the Imperial Rattan Company, of Stratford, Ontario.

Designed by the distinguished Finnish architect, Eliel Saarinen, then president of the Cranbrook Academy of Art, in Michigan, this extensive line of tables, cabinets, beds, and upholstered seating made its first public appearance in Simpson's 'Apartments of Today' (figs.108–10). The Saarinen furniture was described as 'simple modern furniture – comfortable and sensible in design, restful and inviting to the eye, scaled to meet the needs of ordinary-sized rooms in today's houses and city apartments, and capable of being produced by factory methods and sold at a reasonable price.'

Made of 'good Canadian birch,' the pieces were finished in a subdued wheat tone, instead of the harsh, glossy surface previously produced by Imperial. The headboards, chests of drawers, cabinets, and open storage units were all the same height so that pieces would be truly interchangeable, and when the line was shown again the next year it was officially called 'Interchangeable Modern.'

It included two suites of furniture in addition to beds and modular cabinetry. The living-room suite comprised a sofa, lounge chair, and side chair in solid birch with 'homespun plaid' upholstery, along with side tables and coffee tables, some with metal tops.[18] The dining-room suite had 'tub shape' dining chairs and a large, round dining table with removable outer leaves. The Simpson's installation of the new furniture, designed by H.L. Deacon of the store's Interior Decorating Department, used pale pinks and dark browns, with touches of turquoise and blue. The walls were described by *Canadian Homes and Gardens* as 'deliberately left plain.'

From 1936 to 1945, the Interior Design department at l'École du Meuble was headed by the Montreal architect Marcel Parizeau, a well-known proponent of Québécois *moderne* design. Parizeau, following the example set by Gauvreau, obtained many building and furniture commissions for himself, and for his fellow teachers and students. (Some work produced at the school was also sold at the end of the academic year to help defray school expenses.) The furniture and cabinetry designed by Parizeau was of a very high standard. He took full advantage of Quebec's craft-based approach to furnishings to fine-tune each client's home and provide special touches of luxury (figs. 111–13). Himself a member of a socially prominent Quebec family, Parizeau was also able to find the patrons and publicity needed to support many progressive endeavours. An extension to l'École du Meuble, designed by Parizeau, was built in 1941.

The Royal Society of Canada published memoirs by the previous director of the school, Jean-Marie Gauvreau, titled *Evolution et tradition des meubles canadiens*.[19]

Fig. 103 Guest room, the Park Plaza Hotel, Toronto. Designed by Hugh G. Holman. Furniture in burled woods by the Andrew Malcolm Company, Kincardine, Ontario (Advertisement, *Canadian Homes and Gardens*, June–July 1936)

Fig. 104 Guest room, the Park Plaza Hotel, Toronto, decorated in chocolate-brown, beige, turquoise, and white. Furniture made in Canada by Kroehler (*Canadian Homes and Gardens*, June–July 1936)

Fig. 105 Guest suite, the Vancouver Hotel, 1939 (Vancouver Public Library/11485)

Fig. 106 (a) Canada Pavilion, 1937 Paris exposition;
(b) Furniture display, the Canada pavilion, 1937 Paris exposition (*Industrial Canada*, November 1937)

Repeating the theme of his 1929 book, *Nos intérieurs de demain*, Gauvreau reaffirmed Quebec's role as 'les héritiers de la culture et des traditions françaises en Amérique.' He argued that American design was principally derived from English design, and that English design was principally derived from French design. Victorian styles were simply Louis XV pieces that had been 'déformées, étirées, triturées' (deformed, stretched, manipulated). To make his point, Gauvreau correctly reminded readers that the United States had not participated in the 1925 Paris exposition because the country's manufacturers had not had 'original' products to show, but misleadingly referred to their 'exclusion' from the exposition, when in fact they had declined a formal invitation.

Gauvreau was writing in 1944, but the only furniture designers mentioned in his purported history and survey of the field were Duncan Phyfe, Emile-Jacques Ruhlmann, Gauvreau himself, and his colleague Parizeau. As for the significance of work being done in other parts of Canada, one had only to ask oneself 's'il préfere Toronto a Montreal? La résponse ne se fera pas attendre' ('Does one prefer Toronto to Montreal? There is no hesitation in answering.')

Fig. 107 Canadian furniture display, the British Industries
Fair, Earl's Court, London, 1938 (*Industrial Canada*, April 1938)

Fig. 108 Living-room furniture: birch, upholstery. Designed by Eliel Saarinen, Cranbrook Academy of Art, Michigan. Manufactured by the Imperial Rattan Company, Stratford. Displayed at Robert Simpson Company, Toronto (*Canadian Homes and Gardens*, April 1941)

Modern Furniture in Canada

Fig. 109 Dining-room furniture: birch, upholstery. Designed by Eliel Saarinen, Cranbrook Academy of Art, Michigan. Manufactured by the Imperial Rattan Company, Stratford. Displayed at Robert Simpson Company, Toronto (*Canadian Homes and Gardens*, April 1941)

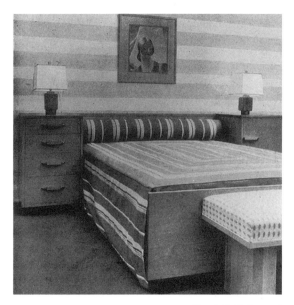

Fig. 110 Bedroom furniture: birch. Designed by Eliel Saarinen, Cranbrook Academy of Art, Michigan. Manufactured by the Imperial Rattan Company, Stratford. Displayed at Robert Simpson Company, Toronto (*Canadian Homes and Gardens*, April 1941)

Fig. 111 Living room in the home of Mr and Mrs Walter
Downs, Montreal. Designed by Marcel Parizeau, Architect
(*Canadian Homes and Gardens*, July 1940)

Fig. 112 Dining room in home of Mr and Mrs Downs,
Montreal. Designed by Marcel Parzeau, Architect
(*Canadian Homes and Gardens*, July 1940)

Fig. 113 Living room in the home of Jean Béique, Montreal.
Designed by Marcel Parizeau, Architect (*Canadian Homes
and Gardens*, October 1943)

Fig. 114 Dining room of the Green Lantern Restaurant, Barrington Street, Halifax, 1941 (Photo: E.A. Bollinger, Photograph Collection, Public Archives of Nova Scotia/231-A)

Fig. 115 Counter area of the Green Lantern Restaurant, Halifax, 1941 (Photo: E.A. Bollinger, Photograph Collection, Public Archives of Nova Scotia/230)

Craft and Design

The Second World War had an immediate impact on Canadian furniture manufacturing. The supply of most materials was restricted. Steel, for example, was no longer available for furniture as there was an insufficient supply for the country's 'immediate war and essential civilian requirements.'[1] Many factories making wood furniture were converted for war production, under contract to the Department of Munitions and Supply.

The furniture industry benefited, however, from expanded and accelerated production in related industries. Canada's first synthetic-rubber plant was built, by the Polymer Corporation, in 1943. (It had the largest steam power plant in the country.) And, in 1944, the Perkins Glue Company of Pennsylvania opened a plant in Kitchener, specifically to supply new types of resin, casein, and vegetable wood glues to Canadian furniture manufacturers. These had been developed in the company's research laboratories for military landing and cargo barges.

Efficiency and durability were emphasized in the furniture that was produced during these years, and frugal resourcefulness on the home front was encouraged by posters displayed in public places and by advertisements in newspapers and magazines. But some towns and cities, such as Halifax, Nova Scotia, benefited from the greatly increased wartime activity (figs. 114 and 115).

New types of modular wood-frame seating and cabinetry components came onto the market. These were modest in appearance and could be bought as needed, or as savings permitted. The first example of the modular furniture in Canada was a line of flexible-unit seating by Snyder's that was displayed in Eaton's Thrift House in 1941 (fig. 116). This seating was promoted for its flexibility and practicality – the upholstery fabric was advertised to be long-wearing, and pieces could be rearranged to suit changing needs 'for maximum usefulness.' Modular furniture was also convenient for the manufacturers – a new decorating idea that did not require any investment in new technologies.

At the end of the war, Canada was the one of the world's leading exporters of manufactured goods. This was a temporarily elevated status, caused by the wartime collapse of European trade, but Canadians hoped that it could somehow be sustained through increased manufacturing output. Governments and industrialists knew that materials and processes developed during the war could be adapted for new products and new profits, while an imminent housing boom would fuel the consumer market (figs. 117 and 118). In Europe and the United States, industrial designers were already playing an important role as manufacturing consultants and as educators. In Canada, however, most manufacturers had demonstrated a remarkable reluctance to invest in design development, and so the profession of industrial design had not yet given birth to itself.

Two young American architects, Eero Saarinen and Charles Eames, won the 'Organic Design' competition held in 1941 by the Museum of Modern Art in New York. Their moulded-plywood furniture was first published in Canada in November 1945 when a photograph of Saarinen and Eames's armchair, dining chair, and modular cabinetry accompanied an article in *Canadian Art* by E.W. Thrift titled 'New Patterns in Industry.' Thrift thought that the home- and office-furnishings industry could 'eventually absorb a large part of our industrial production and output of raw materials.' He discussed the need for design planning, the training requirements of designers, and the need for 'a broad artistic base in the community' to produce talent and support markets. The Canadian home-furnishing industry was, in Thrift's opinion, 'a most backward field in its lack of the use of modern technology.'[2]

In September 1943, a *Canadian Homes and Gardens* article titled 'Furniture Futures' reported on an American survey in which 60 per cent of people interviewed had expressed a preference for modern furniture. The debate in the Canadian press regarding furniture was still very much an either/or issue – one was either for modern design or against it. Every new editor ploughed the same old furrow – 'Does "Contemporary Design" Mean Anything to You?' asked a 1945 headline.[3]

The only journalist who discussed design and fabrication in any detail was Donald Buchanan, Supervisor of Special Projects for the National Film Board of Canada and a founding editor of *Canadian Art* magazine in 1944. This national arts quarterly supported the goals of the Federation of Canadian Artists, which declared at its 1944 annual conference that industrial design should be regarded as a national asset. *Canadian Art*, as a result, included in its coverage not only painting, drawing, and sculpture, but also product design, graphic design, architecture, and craft.

Fig. 116 Sectional seating units manufactured by Snyder's (*Canadian Homes and Gardens*, November 1941)

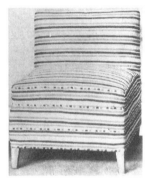

Fig. 117 Cover of *Canadian Affairs* magazine, 1945, published by the Wartime Information Board for distribution to Canadian armed forces. Illustration by Harry Mayerovitch, National Film Board (*Canadian Art*, Summer 1947)

Fig. 118 Rendering of open-plan living and dining area in the 'Help-less' House by Eaton's Interior Decorating Bureau (*Canadian Homes and Gardens*, May 1945)

Fig. 119 Corner of living-room setting, exhibition by the Ontario Branch of the Canadian Handicrafts Guild at the auditorium, Eaton's College Street store, Toronto. Furniture designed by Greta d'Hont, Montreal. Upholstery and drapery fabrics woven by Karen Bulow, Montreal (*Canadian Homes and Gardens*, June 1942)

Fig. 120 American acrylic table on rug woven by Karen Bulow, Montreal. 'Design in Industry' exibition, the Royal Ontario Museum, 1945 (*Canadian Art*, Summer 1945)

New technologies and the respective merits of craft and industrial production were vigorously debated among craftspeople, artists, architects, and bureaucrats. They all saw themselves as the product designers and/or design arbiters of the future. The craft community argued in favour of functional production by independent craftspeople. The arts community proposed a role for artists as design consultants to industry. Architects pushed for large-scale industrial production designed and managed by architects, while bureaucrats wanted to establish regulations about 'good' and 'bad' design. All of these groups energetically defended their existing territories while staking out claims to new ones.

The craft community publicly demonstrated its new interest in design through annual guild exhibitions (fig. 119) and a large, curated exhibition held in Toronto in the summer of 1945. This exhibition, called 'Design in Industry,' was organized by the Ontario section of the Canadian Handicrafts Guild, along with the Royal Ontario Museum. It included fine craft and industrial products from Canada and other countries. The work was installed in realistic settings, showing the interplay of handmade and machine-made objects (fig. 120). The pieces were all functional so as to emphasize the message to manufacturers that Canadian craftspeople had significant potential as designers of mass-produced household goods. An enthusiastic report on the exhibition in *Canadian Homes and Gardens* concluded that the exhibition would 'show the place of the designer craftsman in successful industrial production.'[4]

This opinion was not shared by Donald Buchanan. Writing in *Canadian Art*, he declared that the name of the exhibition,'Design in Industry,' was a 'misnomer' and that the exhibition proved only that, 'in Canada, the promotion of art in industry has a long way yet to go.'[5] Specifically, he thought that the Canadian woodworking was 'adolescent,' that the glass-making needed 'more criticism,' and that the furniture was weak. 'Do our cabinet makers really believe that stolidity is a virtue?' he asked. Buchanan objected to the inclusion of so much handmade work, apparently overlooking the fact that the event had been organized by a craft guild. He accused the exhibition organizers of ignoring what he thought was the really important issue: what new products could be made with 'aluminum sheets, magnesium rods, plywood, chemical plastics and cellulose compounds.' He pointed out that Canadian manufacturers had 'developed new techniques of design for use in war that can be applied in peace as well' and suggested that it was that 'sort of thing which should be the keynote of any truly contemporary exhibition of industrial art.'

The advanced moulding techniques developed for plywood and aluminum in airplane manufacturing proved to be of great value to the furniture industry. Five Ontario furniture factories, including Imperial Rattan, had been converted for the production of components for Mosquito bombers and Avro Anson trainers. After the war, several of these manufacturers applied their new moulding expertise to the production of plywood furniture. The Canadian Wooden Aircraft Company, in Stratford, was the first to successfully introduce moulded wood to the consumer residential market. The company's designs were developed by two Polish airmen, W. Czerwinski and H. Stykolt, who had worked for the Canadian Wooden Aircraft

Company designing and making plywood components for the Mosquito. Their line of furniture included a dining table, dining chair, and two armchairs (fig. 121), made of bent laminated wood and moulded plywood, inspired by the 1930s designs of the Finnish architect Alvar Aalto. At some point during, or just after, the war, the Canadian Wooden Aircraft Company became a division of Imperial Rattan.

Czerwinski and Stykolt's furniture was displayed in an exhibition organized by the Art Gallery of Toronto, 'Design in the Household,' which opened in January 1946. The exhibition was organized by the gallery's curator (later director), Martin Baldwin, and it included pieces from the annual exhibition of the same name at the Museum of Modern Art in New York. These were augmented by a wide range of Canadian products. At a conference the previous summer, Baldwin had explained to an audience of manufacturers that the purpose of the exhibition was to 'educate purchasing demand.'[6] The exhibition was officially opened by W.F. Holding, chairman of the Toronto Branch of the Canadian Manufacturers' Association. Holding said that he did not 'subscribe to the view held by some' that products made in Canada should be instantly recognizable as being Canadian. Rather, one should take the 'best from the past or from the inspiration of other countries.'

Holding was followed by the president of the gallery, C.S. Band, a manufacturer of rubber and plastic products. In his address, which, like Holding's, was informative and enlightened, Band said that Canada had to give more attention to design so as to sell goods in 'a competitive post-war world.' He continued: 'Articles mass-produced, for a very large market, tend to be more conservative in design than those produced in smaller quantities for a more restricted trade but the latter often set the standard towards which mass-production eventually strives.'[7] A large introductory panel at the entrance to 'Design in the Household' explained that the 'purposes of the exhibition' were:

- To show that our natural resources plus the possibilities of the machine make possible mass-production that should lead to right equipment for living.

- To describe and illustrate the essential elements of design in useful objects.

- To illustrate design with examples suited to the household.

The exhibition occupied five galleries and showed hundreds of products displayed under such headings as 'The Designer Knows Material' and 'Expression of the Designer Completed.' One panel, headed simply 'The Designer,' declared that 'since the beginning of recorded history the fine designer craftsman has created standards to which all others must aspire.'

The furniture displayed was quite modest but generated a great deal of interest from the public, as 16,000 people visited the exhibition during its first three weeks. Many left sceptical remarks in the comments and questions boxes provided by the gallery. 'Why are all the modern designs American?' asked one. Others described the Canadian pieces as 'too small,' 'too plain,' 'inferior,' and 'impractical,' while the

Fig. 121 Armchair: moulded plywood, bent laminated wood. Designed by W. Czerwinski and H. Stykolt. Manufactured by the Canadian Wooden Aircraft Company, Stratford, Ontario (*Royal Architectural Institute of Canada Journal*, September 1946)

exhibition itself was observed to be 'poorly displayed' and in need of 'greater conti-nuity.' But most visitors agreed with the gallery's premise that the exhibits were 'edu-cational,' and therefore 'good,' and that the gallery should 'do this type of show again.'[8] The two most frequent comments, however, were 'too modern' and 'too expensive.'

The style of the exhibition was awkwardly didactic. In contrast to the carefully art-directed settings of the guild exhibition at the Royal Ontario Museum, the Art Gallery of Toronto's exhibition looked like a large school-project book, with many panels of educational text. The installation of the objects themselves was even less inspiring, and the overall standard of exhibition design did little to support the gallery's efforts to become a national centre of design advocacy (fig. 122).

The overtly educational nature of the gallery installation was perhaps intended to emphasize Canada's efforts to catch up with industrial design in other countries. The consolidation of Canada's export trade was seen by many to depend on the standard of domestic design (fig. 123). The architect Hazen Sise, writing in the *RAIC Journal*, exlained that 'you cannot use ... plywood with proper effect unless you are willing to adopt the "functional" aesthetic – unless you are willing to use the material honestly and straightforwardly, eschewing the peculiarly Canadian pas-sion for trying to make something look like something else. The export trade may seem like a backstairs way of popularizing modern aesthetics, but public discussion of aesthetics *per se* is a strangely unrewarding activity.'

Donald Buchanan now followed up his published attack on the 'Design in Industry' exhibition at the Royal Ontario Museum by organizing his own exhibi-tion, which would open at the National Gallery and then tour the country. Emphasizing his contempt for the previous effort, Buchanan used the same name, 'Design in Industry.' He prepared for his self-appointed role as national design bureaucrat by spending the first nine months of 1946 organizing and analysing a survey of product design across the country. This research, as well as his subsequent exhibition, was jointly supported by the National Research Council of Canada, the National Gallery, and the National Film Board.

During the course of his research, Buchanan delivered a paper to a conference on reconstruction and economic development held in Toronto.[9] He said that the exhibitions at the museum and the art gallery had included 'some fine pieces' but they had had no relevance to what he called 'the Canadian possibilities.' 'What are the raw materials?' he asked, '[what are] the skills we, as Canadians, are best endowed with?' And how could manufacturers be encouraged to make best use of these skills and materials with the help of Canadian designers?

Buchanan's 'Design in Industry' exhibition opened in October 1946 at the National Gallery, in Ottawa, where he had been made chief of the new Indus-trial Design Section. The exhibition was a collaborative effort involving the National Gallery, the Department of Reconstruction and Supply, and the National Re-search Council. The construction and assembling of the exhibition was done by the Special Projects Unit of the National Film Board, and the exhibition was opened by C.D. Howe, minister of reconstruction. Buchanan used the phrase 'design for the mil-

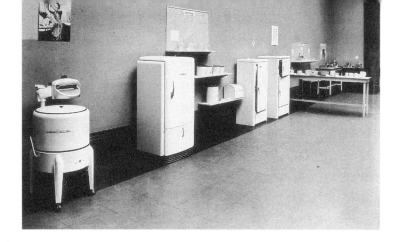

Fig. 122 'Design in the Household' exhibition, the Art Gallery of Toronto, 1946 (Photo: Pringle & Booth, Art Gallery of Ontario Archives)

Fig. 123 Desk chair: moulded plywood and bent laminated wood. Designed by Kenneth Reed. Made by Canada Cabinets and Furniture, Kitchener, Ontario, 1946. Plywood components developed by Bury Lumber, Toronto (Photo: William Deacon, Toronto, 1985)

Fig. 124 Prototype for world's first moulded-plastic chair. Glass fibre–reinforced cotton, synthetic-resin adhesives. Stacking auditorium chair, designed by architects A.J. Donahue and D. Simpson, the National Research Council of Canada, Ottawa. From the Plastics section of 'Design in Industry' exhibition, Ottawa, 1946 (National Archives of Canada/PA-160515)

Fig. 125 Design for stacking
auditorium chair in moulded plastic,
by architects A.J. Donahue and D.
Simpson (*Canadian Art*, February 1947)

Fig. 126 Prototype for moulded chair by Donahue and
Simpson on display in the Plastics section of 'Design in
Industry' exhibition, Ottawa, 1946 (National Archives of
Canada/PA-160509)

lions' to capture the goal of the exhibition, much of which was later seen in installations at Morgan's department store in Montreal and at Eaton's in Toronto. Only Canadian-made products were shown, including some industrial products, such as porcelain insulators, along with laboratory glassware, furniture, lighting, appliances, kitchen utensils, hardware, and sporting equipment.

The Plastics section of the 'Design in Industry' exhibition featured a design for the world's first moulded-plastic chair (figs. 124–6), a stacking auditorium chair developed during 1945 and 1946 in the Structures Laboratory of the National Research Council, in Ottawa. The chair and table displayed were made of ten layers of glass fibre–reinforced cotton, 3/16 of an inch in total thickness, moulded onto a reusable form with epoxy-resin adhesives, and baked in an autoclave at 350 degrees Centigrade. (The epoxy resins had been developed during the war for the Mosquito bomber.) It had a light grey, glossy finish, and was fire and acid resistant.

The chair was designed for the National Research Council by two architects, A.J. Donahue and Douglas C. Simpson. Jim Donahue, who was born in Regina, Saskatchewan, in 1918, obtained his Bachelor of Architecture degree at the University of Minnesota, and then completed his Master's degree at Harvard University in 1942. There he studied under the illustrious Bauhaus architects Walter Gropius and Marcel Breuer. Donahue's familiarity with the prefabricated-housing systems developed by Gropius with Konrad Wachsmann enabled him to obtain a job in Ottawa working on prefabricated-housing structures for the Building Research Division of the National Research Council (NRC). His parallel interest in materials applications would have been encouraged by his studies under Breuer, who had been a furniture pioneer in the use of bent steel tube in the 1920s, and of moulded plywood in the 1930s. In 1945, Donahue designed and curated a national touring exhibition, with Donald Buchanan, called 'Wood in Canada.'

Douglas Simpson was born in Winnipeg, Manitoba, in 1916, and graduated as an architect from the University of Manitoba in 1938. After serving with the Royal Canadian Navy during the war, he worked as an architect in Ottawa, and as a researcher at the NRC Building Research Division, where he recruited Donahue for the chair project. Simpson and Donahue applied for a patent for the chair, but their application was refused, and the design was not put into production.[10] The NRC engineer for the plastic-furniture project was Eric Brown.

Donahue and Simpson left Ottawa to pursue their architecture careers, in Winnipeg and Vancouver, respectively. The first mass-produced moulded-plastic chair was developed three years later, in 1949, by the American architect/designer Charles Eames. His 1949 prototype consisted of a plastic seat shell attached to a steel base. It was displayed for the first time in 1950, in an exhibition at the Museum of Modern Art in New York. This exhibition was the result of an international competition for 'Low Cost Furniture' sponsored by the museum in 1948. The group of life-size models originally submitted to the competition by Eames and his team had actually been made of moulded metal sprayed with neoprene, a synthetic rubber, to simulate the appearance of plastic.[11] The ambitious one-piece Donahue/Simpson design of

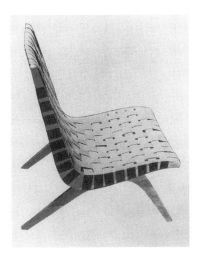

Fig. 127 Lounge chair: plywood, canvas webbing. Designed by architect A.J. Donahue (*Design for Use in Canadian Products*, Ottawa, 1947)

Fig. 128 Plywood section of the 'Design in Industry' exhibition, Ottawa, 1946 (National Archives of Canada/ PA-168138)

Fig. 129 Still from the film *Better Design for Everyday Use, ca* 1951. Dining chairs in moulded plywood and bent laminated wood. Manufactured by the Canadian Wooden Aircraft Company, Stratford (National Archives of Canada/National Film Board of Canada/PA-183066)

1946 was three years in advance of the two-piece Eames prototypes for MOMA, and sixteen years ahead of the first mass-produced one-piece plastic chair, a school chair designed by Marco Zanuso and Richard Sapper for the Municipality of Milan, Italy, in 1961, and manufactured by Kartell.

Photographs of the 'Design in Industry' exhibition were published in a small book called *Design for Use in Canadian Products*, which was a survey of 'design in Canada of manufactured goods for the home and office, for sports and outdoors.'[12] The cover featured a simple birch plywood chair designed by Donahue (fig. 127). The text, written by Buchanan, urged that 'a method ... be found of establishing proper channels of communication between ... manufacturers and Canadian designers,' perhaps through design competitions, and that more attention be paid to design education. The only area in which Buchanan thought that Canada was a leader was in the design of kitchen equipment, but he also praised the new types of sectional upholstered seating made by Snyder's 'that can be fitted ideally into the restricted space of apartments and small homes.' 'Styling' was just 'superficial modification' and was to be avoided. Industrial design must be concerned with fundamentals – 'to simplify and to speed up production,' saving money, but also bringing 'added clarity of design.' Buchanan called for a national design research centre, commanding 'the joint support of manufacturers and government agencies.' He referred to Britain's recently established Council of Industrial Design as a suitable model to follow. The first step would be to set up a 'central clearing house for the exchange of information' and then initiate financing of 'research in industrial design by joint grants from government and industry.' This would have to be based on 'definite, specific proposals' by industrial groups and educational and government agencies.

Buchanan's exhibition, as well as the book and NFB film based on it, featured moulded-plywood furniture made by the Canadian Wooden Aircraft Company (figs. 128 and 129), first shown at the 'Design in the Household' exhibition at the Art Gallery of Toronto. This publicity brought the furniture to the attention of Archibald King and Balfour Swim, two returned servicemen in Nova Scotia, who visited the company's manufacturing facility in Stratford, Ontario. They then started their own company, Ven-Rez Products, and set up a modern factory, capable of producing 40,000 chairs a year, in an ex-Navy facility in Shelburne, Nova Scotia. The company produced a wide range of commercial and institutional furniture (figs. 130–2), including plywood chairs and tables for many of the new schools built in the Maritimes after the war.[13]

Donald Buchanan was committed to the idea of large-scale industrial production and was an influential promoter of architects as industrial designers and planners. Only architects, he claimed, had the comprehensive, practical training that enabled a designer to 'use more or less standardized parts to meet a client's wishes' and were the experts 'best suited to meet the combined needs of the manufacturer and the consumer.'

Canada's first Industrial Design course was taught in Toronto at the University of Toronto School of Architecture as an elective for third-year students in 1946.[14]

Fig. 130 Schoolroom in Nova Scotia, *ca* 1949. Chairs in moulded plywood and bent laminated wood, tables in solid wood and bent laminated wood. Designed by Archibald King and Balfour Swim. Manufactured by Ven-Rez Products, Shelburne, Nova Scotia (Photo: Jones and Morris, Toronto)

Fig. 131 Room in junior school in Nova Scotia, *ca* 1949. Chairs in moulded plywood and bent laminated wood, tables in solid wood and bent laminated wood. Designed by Archibald King and Balfour Swim. Manufactured by Ven-Rez Products, Shelburne, Nova Scotia (Photo: Jones and Morris, Toronto)

Fig. 132 School gymnasium in Nova Scotia, *ca* 1949.
Chairs in moulded plywood and bent laminated wood.
Designed by Archibald King and Balfour Swim. Manu-
factured by Ven-Rez Products, Shelburne, Nova Scotia
(Photo: Jones and Morris, Toronto)

The school was at that time part of the Faculty of Applied Science and Engineering. In its first two years, the new course included projects relating to gas cooking equipment, based on engineering specifications supplied by Canadian manufacturers, and on the students' analyses of consumer needs. According to Buchanan, 'the young architect or engineer who wished to make a profession of product designing must be a man of considerable imagination ... he must understand his social environment as clearly as he understands the principles of fine form and just proportion.'[15]

The University of Toronto course was quickly followed by the establishment of an Industrial Design program at the Ontario College of Art, which had actually been called the Central Ontario School of Art and Industrial Design before and during the First World War. The new program was set up in 1947 under the direction of an American industrial designer, Charles Wetmore. Wetmore was soon replaced by H.A. Nieboer, whose course description in the school prospectus described Industrial Design as the 'integration between the aesthetic, the functional/technological and the commercial.' Courses in his program included descriptive geometry, clay-modelling, materials, colour, three-dimensional design, public relations, management, and the 'laws of symmetry' (fig. 133). The training was intended to enable graduates to assist Ontario manufacturers in competing against a tidal wave of increasingly sophisticated imported products.

Training in furniture craftsmanship was impeded by the tentative nature of craft education in Canada. In 1945 the president of the Ontario College of Art, F.S. Haines, described the priorities of the school's craft programs as, first, 'the developing of designers for the various crafts and industries'; second, the training of craft teachers; and, third, encouraging adults to take up handicrafts as hobbies.[16] Professional craft programs were routinely compromised by the encouragement of amateur activities in school studios, and there was little or no attempt to train craftspeople to become full-time designer/makers. This affected the ability of the schools to generate the type of multiskilled designer essential for furniture research and development.

The diminishment of the role of fine craft at the Ontario College of Art was particularly ironic in light of its original mandate. The 1919 Act of Incorporation for the newly reorganized school described its purpose as 'the training of students in the fine arts, including drawing, painting, design, modelling and sculpture, and in all branches of the applied arts in the more artistic trades and manufactures.'

The lack of a clear commitment to the independent professional status of craft disciplines made craft education vulnerable to the anti-craft propaganda of postwar industrial boosters. Buchanan sarcastically described the craft courses at the Ontario College of Art as 'patterns for wallpapers and textiles, lettering, leatherwork, and wood-carving.' He insisted that these types of courses 'must be definitely demarcated from the more advanced technical and organisational understanding that must be given students who want to specialize in designing for machine production.'[17] In other words, the teaching of design, which was more advanced, should be cut off from the teaching of crafts, deemed to be less advanced.

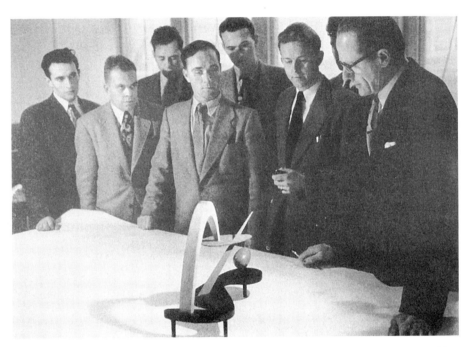

Fig. 133 Industrial Design class with teacher H.A. Nieboer. Ontario College of Art, Toronto, 1949 (Ontario College of Art prospectus, 1950)

What Buchanan and other Canadian industrial design advocates chose not to acknowledge was that surface design, graphic design, fine woodworking – in fact, all the crafts – had significant potential connections to machine production. Although he regularly published photographs of fine craft in *Canadian Art*, Buchanan chose not to discuss the influence of studio crafts on product design and seemed to be unaware of the complex historical relationship between the two fields of endeavour.

Buchanan's writing was criticized on this point by a reader, Deane Russell, of Ottawa, who wrote to *Canadian Art,* signing his letter 'Secretary, Interdepartmental Committee on Arts and Crafts.' Russell reported a 'widely shared feeling of exception' to Buchanan's statement that the application of new materials to household uses had 'more potential value' than the 'encouragement of very minor crafts such as wood carving by amateur craftsmen.' Russell pointed out that, in Sweden, promoters of industrial design recognized that 'their efforts would be incomplete unless comparable efforts were made to encourage the people themselves to participate in design and craft programmes on a national scale.' He warned that 'industrial arts should not be promoted to the exclusion of other creative art and craft interests.'[18]

In a subsequent article that was uncharacteristically supportive of craft, titled 'Fine Craftsmanship and Mass Production,' Buchanan quoted from notes prepared for him by the Montreal weaver Karen Bulow.[19] Bulow, too, praised the situation in Sweden, where craft was 'used as a basis for design in the manufacturing industries.' In Canada 'this great potentiality' was undeveloped. Bulow's attitude, however, was very different from Russell's. As a professional craftsperson, she deplored the fact that crafts were widely regarded as 'hobbies' in Canada, and left 'in the hands of amateurs.' She identified the principal cause of the schism between crafts and fine art and design – that those who worked to raise the standards of Canadian crafts did so 'without support from the government, universities and the public.'[20]

The quality of Canadian craftsmanship was praised in an article titled 'Handicrafts and Industrial Design,' written by Peter Brieger for the April 1945 issue of the international decorative-arts periodical *The Studio*. He described the work he had seen in Canada as 'outstanding' and especially admired textiles and hooked rugs from Quebec and the Maritimes, which he thought were better than any comparable Canadian machine-made products. In furniture, too, he thought that the work of 'individual cabinet makers' was 'far in advance of that of large manufacturers.'

In the late 1940s, people interested in learning the woodworking and metal-working skills needed to make furniture would have entered into unofficial apprenticeships with cabinet-makers and/or studied at technical colleges and night schools. In Toronto they could take the two-year diploma course in Furniture Design, or the upgrading courses in Furniture Crafts, at the Ryerson Institute of Technology (now Ryerson Polytechnic University). By 1949, Ryerson was also offering a two-year diploma course in Interior Design. Perhaps as a reaction to the anti-production conservatism of the Furniture and Cabinet Making course at the Ontario College of Art, Ryerson emphasized the technical nature of its courses. The college advertised that its 'studio shops and laboratories' were modern and well equipped, and that opportunities for 'technological specialization' were provided.[21]

Donald Buchanan had mentioned in 'Design for Use' that l'École du Meuble in Montreal was one of the few schools in Canada that had any sort of connection with industry, although it was in 'a rather restricted local sense.' The school was still devoted to fine craft, but the aesthetic sensibility expressed in the work was often drawn from modern European and American designs for mass production. One member of the faculty, Henri Beaulac, combined these modern influences with his own interest in Louis XVI and Chinese designs, to produce highly eclectic cabinetry and metalwork.

On the West Coast the Vancouver School of Art advertised itself confidently as a school of 'fine and industrial art,' although its official course list referred only vaguely to 'design' and 'handicrafts.' Woodworking, which would have been the likely base for aspiring furniture makers, was not specifically mentioned in the list of courses of any art school in the Western provinces in 1947.[22]

In the Maritimes, crafts were recognized as an important traditional source of income, and governments encouraged craft activities as sustainable cottage industries ideally suited to supplement seasonal resource industries such as agriculture and fishing. Postwar retraining programs invigorated Maritime craft traditions by employing professional craftspeople and designers to teach craft production techniques to returned servicemen and their families. Woodworking courses were offered in New Brunswick at the Saint John Vocational School, and at Mount Allison University, in Sackville, and in Nova Scotia, at the Nova Scotia College of Art, in Halifax. These East Coast endeavours usually promoted designing and making for small-scale craft production. Quebec supported a larger, mixed industry of craft and factory production, while Ontario, Canada's industrial core, continued to stress design for mass production.

Fig. 134 Armchair: bent laminated wood, upholstery.
Manufactured by Mouldcraft Plywoods, Vancouver
(*Canadian Art*, March 1947)

Architects
and Advocacy

A special 'Design in Industry' issue *Journal of the Royal Architectural Institute of Canada* was published in July 1947. In a strongly worded introduction, architect-editor Eric Arthur said that the war had probably 'thrown into the limbo of best forgotten things all that adoration of the foreign expert that drove our good craftsmen and designers abroad.'

He hoped 'no manufacturer was left in Canada who believed ... that his wares should be designed to meet the desires of the lowest common denominator in a moronic, hypothetical section of the Canadian public.' Arthur continued:

> It always strikes us as strange, with a public always on the watch for something new in razors or motor cars, that any manufacturer should feel a well thought out design should be modified because it was a 'jump' ahead of the public ... every designer had had the experience of seeing the vital spark taken out of a design in order to meet a presumed lower standard in a general public which may, in fact, be ahead of the manufacturer in its demands and thinking.

Arthur thought that industrial design offered new professional opportunities for the many war veterans then attending architecture schools, and that this new profession might actually be more financially rewarding than the practice of architecture. In a slightly peevish flight of fancy, probably inspired by stories about the French-American designer Raymond Loewy, Arthur speculated that

> ... the industrial designer ... may, from what we read in *Life*, reach a dizzy financial level in which he will move in a rarified atmosphere peopled by movie stars and steel magnates. He will relax, between designs, on down cushions on the edge of amoeba shaped pools with soft music and a background of his own house. The successful architect on the other hand has none of these luxuries, and is seldom known to live in a house designed for himself.

Arthur's introduction was followed by an article titled 'The World Picture,' by G. Englesmith, who mentioned by name a great many architects, designers, educators, and design movements, including the Deutscher Werkbund, the Bauhaus, and the new American 'Bauhauses' in Chicago and Cambridge. He credited industrial design as the vehicle by which the 'new design philosophy was first accepted by the public,' but chastised industrial designers for attempting to solve architectural problems, extending 'the functional and clean form philosophy of the kitchen to other parts of the building.' From his vantage as an architect and as an instructor at the University of Toronto, Englesmith could see that industrial designers generally failed in architectural work because of their 'lack of education and aesthetic sensibility,' and that this failure was the predictable outcome of the 'unenlightened confidence placed in them by manufacturers and the public.' 'Irresponsible designers ... more interested in the quick upward curve of the sales graph' were 'polluting the market and public taste.'

While relegating industrial designers to the kitchen, Englesmith mapped out a huge territory suitable for intervention by architects. He equated 'a basic philosophy of design' with a 'new age' of creative planning for social, political, and economic structures; regional development; land conservation; and transportation networks. Every aspect of life would come under the scrutiny of those who, like Englesmith, understood the required balance between the rational and the emotional sides of the brain, and could translate this into enlightened design. The photographs that accompanied Englesmith's article were more helpful than the text, covering a wide range of products, including the new moulded-plywood chairs and tables designed by Charles Eames and made by Evans Products, in Venice, California.

'The Canadian Picture,' by Donald Buchanan, commenced with a brisk summation: 'In Canada we have a history of good craftsmanship in certain types of woodworking, of originality in some kinds of handcraft weaving, of skill and invention in engineering; yet we possess few achievements of importance in the design of manufactured goods.' Buchanan went on to note that, by generally accepted definitions of the term 'industrial designer,' there were 'no more than a dozen men so qualified and so experienced in Canada.' The survey that he had conducted prior to the

'Design in Industry' exhibition revealed that 'three out of four sales managers of industrial firms ... understood industrial art to mean merely applied ornamentation.'

Buchanan lamented the fact that furniture manufacturing in Canada, while 'one of our oldest,' was also 'one of our most conservative' industries and that this conservatism extended to the retailers. The upholstered, bent-laminated-wood chair (fig. 134) developed by Mouldcraft Plywoods, in Vancouver, for example, was commissioned by a chain of furniture stores but then ordered in such small numbers that Mouldcraft's equipment could not be used as intended for mass production, and the final chairs were virtually handmade. This was the danger of relying on the local or domestic market. Companies exporting, or attempting to export, their products were more 'aware of the value of the trained designer' in competing with 'well-designed goods from other countries.' The technical design expertise needed by the manufacturers investing in new wood-, metal-, or plastic-moulding equipment was being supplied by in-house engineers and tradesmen, or by 'a few Canadian engineers' who had 'set themselves up independently as product engineers.'

Buchanan took this opportunity to do some follow-up reporting on the 'Design in Industry' exhibition, which had generated a great deal of publicity:

> It stimulated the *Financial Post* into writing three articles and one editorial on the need for Canadian business locating and using more Canadian talent in this field. Many trade magazines wrote similar articles. The journals *Canadian Business* and *Western Business* published illustrated stories and referred at length to the questions raised, while *Manitoba Industrial Topics* went out of its way to devote almost the whole of its April issue to the Exhibition and to the place of the designer in Canadian industry.

The *Montreal Standard*, a national weekly newspaper, had also devoted its 'rotogravure section' to a photo survey of functional design in Canadian products. And yet there were still the same problems: lack of financing for new design and equipment, the branch-plant status of many of the manufacturing facilities which were owned by American companies, and the ease and relatively small expense of buying design licences from American manufacturers. Canadian manufacturers could use these licences to produce American designs and benefit, at no cost, from the advertising of these products in the widely distributed American magazines. As Buchanan noted, 'they [Canadian manufacturers] will continue to go to Detroit, Grand Rapids, or New York to buy the blueprints unless they are made aware ... of the existence of competent Canadian talent in this field.'

Modern Furniture in Canada

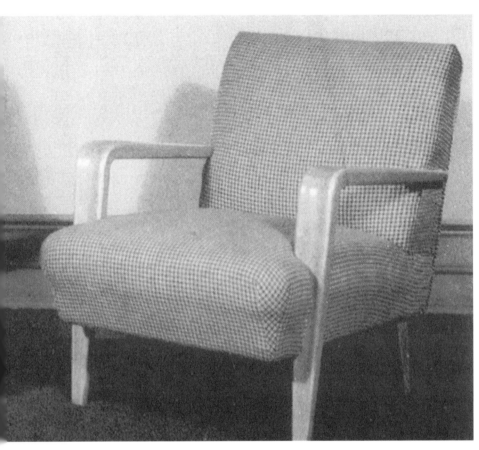

Fig. 135 Sofa and armchair: bent solid wood, solid wood, upholstery. Designed by Donald Strudley, 1947. Manufactured by Imperial Furniture, Stratford. These were among the first pieces of furniture registered in the Canadian 'Design Index,' Ottawa, 1947.

Englesmith had referred in his article to the formation of the Society of American Industrial Designers and the British Council of Industrial Design. Buchanan mentioned the recent establishment of an Affiliation of Canadian Industrial Designers by ten designers from Montreal; Ottawa; Toronto; Winnipeg; and London, Ontario. Seven of the ten were architects, one was an engineer, and most had had their work displayed in the 'Design in Industry' exhibition. A 'mimeographed statement' prepared by this group, and given to manufacturers who visited the exhibition, read, in part: 'While each unit of this affiliation is independent, an attempt nevertheless will be made to pass on to all members of the affiliation such requests for information and advice as are received, so that the individual designer or group in the best position to handle each designing job will be able to undertake it.'

Buchanan envisioned public art galleries operating 'clearing houses for unbiased information' about professional industrial designers, department stores presenting 'intelligent displays devoted to improved designs,' and the establishment of a national design centre housing a design index which would include photographic records of every 'well-designed' product made in Canada. The ostensible purpose of this index would be to provide information about designers to manufacturers. But, as Buchanan pointed out, its benefit 'above all' would be to provide 'a continuous flow of copy and photographs' to editors and writers, such as himself. Buchanan reported that a similar index of American products had been recently initiated at the Albright Art Gallery in Buffalo, New York.[1] The gallery's index was part of its research for a 1947 exhibition, 'Good Design Is Your Business.' The gallery's director, at the time of Buchanan's writing, hoped that this project would lead to the establishment of a permanent industrial design department in the museum, but this did not eventuate. A previous, and better-known, American design index was that established in the mid-1930s as a Federal Art Project; it produced 17,000 full-colour illustrations of decorative, industrial, and vernacular products dating from the founding of the American colony to the end of the nineteenth century.[2]

T.E. Matthews was an industrial designer in the John B. Parkin architectural office in Toronto. He had worked in London, and at Raymond Loewy's Chicago office. His article in this special issue of the *RAIC Journal* echoed Arthur's charge that Canadian architects were interested in industrial design mainly because of 'stories of high fees paid to American designers.' He felt that it would be very hard for these designers to compete against American products, American trends, and American advertising, and that the solution was for them to 'evolve design characteristics' that were 'distinctly Canadian.' He looked to manufacturing associations to assume some of the cost of setting up new schools and expanding existing schools to train this new type of nationally distinctive designer. Matthews also sought to reassure the famously reluctant Canadian manufacturer/client by admonishing designers to make themselves 'keenly aware of public opinion,' so that their designs 'will not be sufficiently startling in character as to create buyer prejudice, thereby greatly reducing sales.'

In 'The Canadian Industrialist's Picture,' Charles Moffat, head of the New Development Division of Moffats Limited, in Weston, Ontario, questioned the suitability of architects as industrial designers. In a polite but firm rebuff to his publisher's and fellow writers' proposals, he suggested that the architectural profession's most important contribution to the field had been the stimulation of 'consumer interest in design.' Moffat thought that architects were not sufficiently familiar with 'the problems of design in the various specialized industrial fields' or with 'the complexity and broadness of the designer's problems within these given industries.' He also felt that the eagerness in Canada to use architects as surrogate industrial designers indicated 'that we have not yet grasped the implications involved.' Moffat praised the Canadian consumer, who, he said, had 'more taste than cash' and was less interested in what a manufacturer 'puts into the product' than in 'what he can get out of' it. 'The manufacturer requires a designer who takes into consideration the consumer's thinking and needs, who is able to feel the pulse and trends in product development and relate these to constantly changing factors – factors in relation to research and engineering, new processes, new materials, machines, transportation and mode-of-living.'

This issue of the *RAIC Journal* was a turning-point in the public stance of the architectural profession towards the practice of industrial design – products and processes were now legitimate areas of study. And the graphic design of this issue set a new standard for the presentation of such material in Canada. In his editorial, Eric Arthur expressed the conviction that this was 'the most useful and successful of the special issues' that the journal had produced.

The Affiliation of Canadian Industrial Designers was established in 1946 by architects Jim Donahue and Douglas Simpson, designers of the National Research Council moulded-plastic chair, along with eight other professional architects and designers, including E.W. Thrift, of Winnipeg; Watson Balharrie, of Ottawa; John B. Parkin and George Englesmith, of Toronto; Leo Skidmore, of London, Ontario; and Henry Finkel and Jacques Bieler, of Montreal. Shortly after, Buchanan's hoped-for 'Design Index' was established, although his initial proposals to the federal government had met with significant oppposition from James McKinnon, the minister of trade and commerce, and C.D. Howe, the minister of reconstruction and supply. Both had 'reacted unfavourably' to the idea of a national index, as this type of centralized registration system could easily, and justifiably, be seen as government meddling with industry.[3] The National Research Council also declined to involve itself in this curatorial/promotional exercise. An industrial design information service was eventually established as an ancillary department of the National Gallery of Canada.

This was the Industrial Design Information Division, set up in June 1947 and managed by Buchanan. In June of the next year, Buchanan organized the National Industrial Design Committee, which selected products for the new 'Design Index' (fig. 135). Continuing the flurry of activity, on 14 October 1948, the Association of Canadian Industrial Designers was established, through letters patent signed by the under-secretary of state for Canada. The petitioning letter for the charter was signed by six designers and three senior University of Toronto administrators – Vincent Massey, chancellor; H. Madill, head of the School of Architecture; and E. Allcut, head of the Department of Mechanical Engineering.[4]

In the Christmas 1947 issue of *Canadian Art*, Buchanan expressed his hope that the 'Design Index' would elevate Canada to the level of other countries where new products were regularly published in art and architecture journals and exhibited in museums. The first Canadian 'Design Index' products published were a steel desk lamp by Crown Electric Company, in Brantford, Ontario; an aluminum water pitcher designed by the Aluminum Company of Canada, in Etobicoke, for Aluminum Goods Limited, of Toronto; and lathe-turned bowls and plates in birch by Habitant Woodworks, in Quebec City. These had apparently passed the test of ten critical 'Design Index' questions relating to 'Form and Commodity,' 'Production,' and 'Originality.' The questions were:

- Is the form suitable to the functions of the object?

- Is there a harmonious relationship of all parts?

- Is the design as simple as it can be?

- Is there a complete absence of all unnecessary or meaningless ornament?

- Is the use of texture and colour both honest and logical in relation to the material used and the function of the object?

- Is it mechanically efficient?

- Is the material used the most suitable in regard to the function of the object and the manufacturing processes used?

- Is it strongly constructed and durable and safe?

- Has ease of maintenance and repair been considered?

- Is the design original, or if an adaptation, is the adaptation both logical and original?[5]

A subsequent article, in the 1948 spring–summer issue, explained the organization of the index in more detail. There were five official categories of production: engineering, light engineering, machine-made goods, factory-made goods with a craft basis, and custom-built or handcraft designs. Furniture was split into two categories: 'machine-made goods,' for moulded or stamped metal or plastic, and 'factory-made with craft basis,' for all other furniture. This article was accompanied by photos of a record cabinet in oak by Canada Cabinets and Furniture, of Kitchener, Ontario; a screen in white oak by a Toronto architect, W.J. McBain; and a metal lamp designed by Ridpath's Limited, in Toronto. These, and other products on the index, were shown in the Manufacturers' Building at that summer's Canadian National Exhibition in Toronto.

The Toronto architectural firm of John B. Parkin had been the most active in seeking commissions for industrial design work, describing themselves as architects and industrial designers on their company letterhead. A new partner in the firm, John C. Parkin (no relation), wrote a feature article for the *RAIC Journal* in June 1948 titled 'The Case for Modern Furniture.' Parkin had studied at the University of Manitoba, and at Harvard under Gropius and Breuer. He had also worked briefly the previous summer in New York for Walter Dorwin Teague, the first president of the Society of American Industrial Designers. Parkin echoed the battle-cry against the manufacturers, attacking the 'backwardness of the industry' and the 'anachronistic character of its products.' He thought that a large part of the problem was the 'diffuse nature of the industry,' with its huge number of mainly small factories suffering from what he saw as a lack of leadership. He compared this with the automobile industry, where a small number of major manufacturers were able 'to pass the reduced manufacturing costs resulting from complete mass-production on to the consumer.'

Parkin credited Eames with making tubular-steel furniture 'palatable' again, after its loss of 'dignity' and 'respectability' through indiscriminate exploitation of Breuer's original, brilliant ideas by 'a host of beverage rooms, barber shops and beauty parlors on three continents.' Parkin revealed his architectural bias by stating that 'theoretically, it is desirable that all new homes have as much built-in furniture as possible.' Because of high costs, however, this was an option for only the 'most fortunate.' For everyone else, he thought, the new lightweight plywood Eames furniture and the sectional or modular cabinetry should be the answer.[6]

Parkin called for the National Research Council to commit itself to continuing furniture-design research if 'private capital' could not, or would not, 'supply the funds.' The creation of such a research and development budget would be a 'fitting complement to the Council's present appropriation for low cost housing research.' The 'securing' of low-cost furniture was necessary not only for new homemakers and 'thousands of veterans' but also for the 'dozens of factories across the nation, situated in small towns, whose existence is ... dependent on the continued prosperity of the furniture industry.' Despite such earnest advocacy, however, the contribution of furniture manufacturing to Canada's national trade and industry was not adequately reflected in either public or private funding for research and development.

In an article titled 'Completing the Pattern of Modern Living' (fig. 136) in *Canadian Art* in the spring of 1949, Buchanan announced that a booklet was being published by the National Gallery which would have photographs of 'over eighty' items entered during the previous two years into the 'Design Index.' Buchanan said that 'certain fairly rigorous tests' had been set by an advisory committee of industrial designers and architects, the National Industrial Design Committee. Hundreds of products had been submitted, but most had been rejected 'because they lacked those qualities of clarity of form, of distinction in colour and finishing, of absence of meaningless ornament, which would have enabled them to come up to the standards set.'

Fig. 136 Illustration accompanying article by Donald Buchanan in *Canadian Art* (Spring 1949)

Fig. 137 Industrial design display at the Canadian National Exhibition, Toronto, 1948. Organized by the National Gallery of Canada and the School of Architecture, University of Toronto. Designed by architect George Englesmith (*Canadian Art*, Spring 1949)

The publication was called *canadian designs for everyday use*. It included photographs of sixty-two products, of which six were furniture. The other items included metal lamps and light fixtures, metal and glass tableware and cookware, stoves, heaters, agricultural and industrial equipment, toys, a tractor, a bus, and a canoe. In the booklet's introduction, Buchanan reported that the National Industrial Design Committee was made up of 'manufacturers, retailers, research officials, educationists and designers.' These participants were united by 'an enthusiasm to co-operate in making sure that Canadian industry will be in a position to meet our increasing desires for better and pleasanter goods, desires which are widespread today, wherever consumer demands are related to rising standards of living.' Buchanan was unabashedly confident about his own criteria for 'good design.' He loathed much contemporary American design, which he dismissed as 'styling' and blamed on American advertising agencies. Canadians, he later wrote, 'are less impressed by chromium plating, flashing lights and ringing bells.'[7]

Buchanan's writing reveals no doubts about the legitimacy of his multifaceted role as bureaucrat/curator/journalist/publicist, and shows no hesitation at laying down the rules for Canadian designers. While his selection of material was thorough and of a high standard, Buchanan's attempts to define correct and incorrect design were often misguided. For example, in this booklet, he spelled out a list of rules, in the form of questions, relating to design and production, including the following:

- Is there a harmonious relationship of all parts? (This implies that no part or section be overemphasized or dramatized at the expense of the object as a whole.)

- Is the design as simple as it can be?

Such rigid conditions would have excluded many beautiful and effective pieces of modern furniture from Buchanan's index, including Eileen Gray's one-armed 'non-conformist' chair of 1929 and Marcel Breuer's visually complex Wassily chair of 1926.

Buchanan appeared to be unaware of the great variety of design work being done in the late 1940s in Europe and elsewhere. His fixed points of reference were a handful of American, English, and Swedish designers, and his parameters were largely limited to the types of work he had seen at the time of his aesthetic awakening in the Sweden pavilion at the 1935 international exhibition in Brussels. Buchanan had spent a few hours there studying 'a choice but small grouping of furniture, kitchenware, glassware and pottery' and was 'thoroughly converted to the modern movement in design.'[8]

His approach to modern design, however, was reductive and dogmatic. Products weren't just selected for the index – they were deemed 'worthy of inclusion.' His tone, typical of much design advocacy of the period, was a remnant of the good

Modern Furniture in Canada

design/bad design instruction used between the wars to establish a coherent public framework for modern theory and practice. By the end of the 1940s, however, this sermonizing was out of sync with the upbeat mood of the magazines and retail stores.

Students from the Industrial Design course at the University of Toronto School of Architecture were recruited to help in the planning and installation of an exhibition based on the *canadian designs for everyday use* booklet. This project was organized by the National Gallery in Ottawa, and first shown at the Canadian National Exhibition in Toronto in the summer of 1948 (fig. 137). It included many items from the 'Design Index,' and one section of the exhibition invited the public to judge the merits of two parallel groups of objects – one group modern and the other traditional. *Canadian Art* reported that visitors 'flocked to the attractive display' and that the design quiz, titled 'A Chance to Test Your Taste,' was a great success. More than 10,000 people stopped to record their votes for what they thought were the best designs.[9] Participants answered questions relating to their preferences in products, and then matched their answers against those of a panel of 'experts.' The quiz display was 'besieged by continuous throngs,' and 'young and old, rich and poor' marked their choices.

There were twelve categories of household objects in the quiz, ranging from door handles to easy chairs. Apparently only a small percentage of the public came close to choosing the same list as the experts. Almost everyone was in agreement, however, about the best of the three lamps in the quiz. This was a simple, adjustable metal lamp that *Canadian Art* reported could not be found for sale in either Ontario or Quebec. The magazine concluded that 'sales managers' standards' were being forced on the consumer, who had 'no power of individual choice.' Consumers in several other provinces had a chance to see the new products for themselves when the exhibition travelled during the following year to the Art Association in Montreal, the Winnipeg Art Gallery, the Saskatoon Art Centre, the Hudson's Bay store in Edmonton, and the Vancouver Art Gallery. In Vancouver, the exhibition was augmented by a display of 'goods of merit produced in British Columbia,' sponsored by the newly formed British Columbia Industrial Design Committee.[10]

The 'Designs for Everyday Use' exhibition also included industrial design projects by students at four Canadian schools of architecture. Post-graduate scholarships were awarded by the federal government to five of these students, from the University of Toronto and the University of Manitoba. The scholarships were specifically given for 'advanced training in product design' at the Illinois Institute of Design, in Chicago, and photographs were later published of projects completed by these students while in Chicago (figs. 138 and 139).[11]

An adventurous and entertaining approach to design and design advocacy was demonstrated through an important exhibition sponsored in 1949 by the Vancouver Community Arts Council. The 'Design for Living' exhibition, held at the Vancouver Art Gallery, brought new designs and design issues to the community through a whimsical and affectionate study of the private lives of four imaginary Vancouver families.[12] The Peridot family needed a living room that could double as a library for

Fig. 138 Chair maquette: moulded and folded cardboard. Designed by Canadian students studying at the Institute of Design, Chicago, on scholarships awarded by the National Industrial Design Committee, *ca* 1951 (National Archives of Canada/National Film Board of Canada/PA-183065)

Fig. 139 (a) Armchair maquette: (b) moulded cardboard and (c) metal. Designed by Canadian students, including Joan Robinson, studying at the Institute of Design in Chicago on scholarships awarded by the National Industrial Design Committee (*Canadian Art*, Christmas 1950)

Fig. 140 Plywood furniture designed by architect Duncan McNab. 'Design for Living' exhibition, the Vancouver Art Gallery, 1949. Organized by the Vancouver Community Arts Council (*Canadian Homes and Gardens*, July 1950)

an academic father and as a weaving space for mother Ruth, who wove 'her house-hold linen out of Canadian flax.' The McTavishes wanted a combined recreation room and workshop for their many hobbies. The Rathburn family, who had received a 'small, Emily Carr canvas' as a wedding present, needed lots of space for house plants, a rock collection, and a mother-in-law. The Saterians were 'sophisticated young people' who wanted an expandable house and a nice setting for their frequent musical evenings and famous buffet suppers. Their living room had to be equally appropriate for a B.C. Binning painting and some inherited furniture.

The proposed homes for these families were presented in interior and exterior architectural renderings, in detailed plans of the houses and gardens, and in custom-made room installations (fig. 140). Illustrated, itemized lists of furnishings were prepared, showing the designer, supplier, materials, and price. The furniture designers were Bob Calvert, Duncan McNab, Catherine Wisnicki, Murray Dunne, and Peter Thornton. Fabricators included D.B. Smith (cabinetry), the Vancouver Vocational Institute (woodwork), Gar-Ken Boats (metalwork), and N. Nelson and Company (upholstery).

This was an ambitious project, linking architects and landscape architects with craftspeople and artists to show the cumulative benefits of conscientious domestic design. Leavened with humour and down-to-earth civic pride, the 'Design for Living' exhibition was an unprecedented, and subsequently unmatched, exercise in enlight-ened collaboration. The sponsor of the project, the Community Arts Council, had been formed in 1946 to implement the recommendations of a report titled *Arts and Our Town*. This report was commissioned by the Junior League of Vancouver and the Community Chest, and was the 'first such report presented to any city in North America.'[13] It aimed to establish a link between social problems in the poorer parts of the city and the lack of cultural activities in those areas, and made many recommendations to alleviate these failures. The aim of the Community Arts Council was to develop healthy minds in new, healthy, suburban settings. As the 'Design for Living' exhibition catalogue said: 'Good design is essential to better living, and better living improves the standard of the entire community.'

The exhibition broke the Vancouver Art Gallery's attendance records and received a great deal of enthusiastic publicity. *Canadian Homes and Gardens* devoted a four-part series to the proposed homes for the Vancouver families under the general heading 'By Canadians For Canadians.'[14] The project was praised for showing 'some of the best thinking of our times' on homes and home furnishings. The first of the four articles listed the three most important organizing principles demonstrated in these theoretical projects:

1. Free time for mother and her helpers – gained in worksaving kitchens and easy-to-keep gardens, by planned storage space and quickly cleaned surfaces.

2. Free space for individual hobbies and family projects – snatched from use-less hallways and seldom used dining rooms, or borrowed from outdoors.

Fig. 141 Furniture designed by architect Bob Calvert: fir plywood, solid wood, webbing, upholstery. 'Design for Living' exhibition, the Vancouver Art Gallery, 1949 (*Canadian Homes and Gardens*, April 1950)

3. Free atmosphere for easing tensions, broadening perspectives – com-
pounded of unpretentious design, sunshine, greenery or a view, and the
considerate separation of noisy work, play, and service areas from calm
places for relaxation (outdoors in summer), and the quiet privacy of
sleeping rooms.

One of the chairs in the exhibition was an inexpensive plywood lounge chair
with canvas webbing designed by architect Bob Calvert of the Vancouver firm Sharp
and Thompson, Berwick, Pratt (fig. 141). *Canadian Homes and Gardens* announced
that the plans for the Calvert chair were available from the architects' office for $2.
This was in keeping with the goals of the Community Arts Council, which stressed
home-based and studio crafts. The organizers of the 'Design for Living' exhibition
took full advantage of Vancouver's limited but varied resources, setting an unusual
example of knowledgeable enthusiasm and practical cooperation.

Fig. 142 Still from film *Better Design for Everyday Use*, National Film Board *ca* 1951. Garden chair in aluminum tube and canvas, designed by B.F. Harber, made by Harber Manufacturing, Fort Erie (National Film Board of Canada, National Archives of Canada/PA-183067)

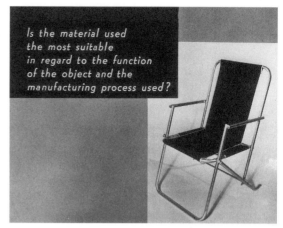

Is the material used the most suitable in regard to the function of the object and the manufacturing process used?

Fig. 143 House of Gordon Farrell, West Vancouver, designed by architects Semmens and Simpson, with chairs by Harber (*Royal Architectural Institute of Canada Journal*, November 1952)

Committees, Competitions, and Commissions

The National Industrial Design Committee issued two publications for manufacturers in 1949. The first, a small leaflet titled *Good Design Will Sell Canadian Products*, was mailed to 6,000 firms.[1] It included a reply card to request further information, which was returned by 1,000 of the recipients. They received a larger brochure titled *How the Industrial Designer Can Help You in Your Business*. This was written specifically for manufacturers, engineers, and technicians. In a foreword, C.D. Howe, now the minister of trade and commerce, warned that Canada would not be able to maintain its level of export activity if it did not improve the quality of its product design. The brochure contained an illustrated section showing how Canadian designers had dealt with five specific projects – a new electric plug, a fan, a chair, a radio, and a tractor. Photographs of drawings and models were featured along with the final products. The text, probably written by Buchanan, emphasized that the industrial designer is a 'MEMBER OF A PLANNING TEAM' who must work with 'plant foremen, sales experts and cost accountants.'

In 1950 the committee commissioned a national survey of the furniture industry by John Low-Beer, of Granby, Quebec, and James Ferguson, of London, Ontario.

They interviewed 'key retailers' as well as 139 manufacturers in 'dozens of furniture-making centres in Ontario and Quebec.'[2] Low-Beer and Ferguson concluded that there was considerable room for improvement in the design of Canadian furniture. Manufacturers were reluctant to risk investment in new designs, even though they enjoyed considerable tariff protection. The retailers were not reliable customers because they were too easily tempted by competing American products. And the buyers were 'generally interested in modern furniture,' although sales of reproduction styles were still very strong.[3] The report found that too many manufacturers were wasting time and energy making frequent, minor changes to their designs, and that too few employed full-time designers.

The report also pointed to a correlation between architectural practice and furniture design. The predominance of modern new homes in British Columbia had produced a healthy market there for modern furniture (figs. 142 and 143). In the Maritimes, there was very little modern housing, and so shoppers showed a marked preference for traditional styles. Most of the manufacturers who participated in the survey piously agreed 'the time had come when the preparation of new designs should be seriously considered' and many were reported to be 'already actively engaged in making such changes.' Low-Beer and Ferguson recommended expansion or amalgamation of existing Canadian design courses and more scholarships for Canadian students to attend American design schools.

Russell Spanner was a young Toronto designer and ex–Ryerson student whose family owned Spanner Products, a woodworking and furniture factory on downtown Elm Street, not far from the Ryerson campus. Spanner worked in the factory during the day and, at night, used its materials and equipment for his own projects, with the collusion of the foreman and the support of his uncle, Oliver Spanner. Russell's father, Albion, was reluctant to change the company's products but, after promoting Russell to foreman in 1948, he allowed him to develop an ambitious new line of armchairs, dining chairs, coffee tables, dining tables, and cabinets (figs.144–7). These modern pieces, marketed as 'Ruspan,' were significantly better than the undistinguished kitchen furniture previously produced by the firm, and represented a conscientious and energetic attempt to invigorate the local furniture industry, which Spanner thought 'wasn't so hot.'[4]

One of Spanner's first designs, an extendable dining table, was shown as an example of good product design in a 1951 article by Buchanan titled 'Good Design or "Styling" – The Choice Before Us.'[5] As well as looking more up-to-date than most Canadian furniture, the new Spanner products were built to last. Russell, a champion amateur wrestler and a big man, liked to demonstrate the strength of his furniture in the Thonet advertising tradition – by standing on it.[6] Spanner's furniture arrived just in time for the postwar building boom and was instantly successful, selling across the country at Eaton's, Simpson's, and many smaller stores, and widely advertised by retailers. The first range of pieces was called the 'Originals,'[7] while two subsequent lines were 'Catalina' and 'Pasadena.'

Spanner became a figure of some prominence, participating in design seminars at the University of Manitoba in 1953, attending a National Industrial Design Council

Fig. 144 Armchair: solid birch, bent laminated birch, canvas. Designed by Russell Spanner, 1950. Manufactured by Spanner Products, Toronto (*The Design Index*, published by the National Gallery of Canada, 1951)

Fig. 145 Simpson's advertisement for Ruspan furniture
by Russell Spanner, manufactured by Spanner Products,
Toronto (*Canadian Art*, Spring 1951)

Fig. 146 The Pierce–Caldwell shop, Bloor Street, Toronto,
mid-1950s. Ruspan furniture on display (Photo: Everett
Roseborough, Toronto)

Fig. 147 'Furniture That Adds Up,' modular sections of furniture designed by Russell Spanner, manufactured by Spanner Products, Toronto (*Canadian Homes and Gardens*, April 1954)

conference in Toronto in 1954, and serving on the Advisory Committee for Furniture and Interior Design at Ryerson Institute of Technology from 1951 to 1956.[8] When Spanner Products moved their factory out of downtown Toronto in the late 1950s, and switched from residential furniture to institutional furniture and fixtures, a Toronto store called 'Modernage' advertised a sale of their Spanner inventory. On the first day of the sale, lines of customers had formed by seven o'clock in the morning.[9]

Russell Spanner's designs combined the sharp geometry of tapered legs and bevelled wood edges with the organic look of natural surfaces, such as cotton webbing and cork. Casual but sophisticated, they reflected the contemporaneous work of the Danish designer Jens Risom and the American designer Paul McCobb. Risom's designs were so popular they were manufactured under licence in both the United States and Canada. The rapidly growing interest in Scandinavian design was, for Canadians, part of the accelerating trend away from European influences. The craftsmanship of the Scandinavians was readily admired, while the lifestyle of the Americans was effortlessly emulated. Canadians were now increasingly seen to be North Americans with an international perspective, rather than dislocated British or French.

Francophone Quebec designers continued to be inspired by French architecture and decorative arts, but also showed a new eagerness to participate in the Canadian furniture industry through national design competitions and interprovincial business. Young Québécois designers and progressive manufacturers were eager to upgrade their province's furniture industry (fig. 148), which could no longer rely on its traditional base of 'favourable labour rates, longer working hours and fresh lumber resources.'[10] Quebec produced a 'much higher proportion of low-priced merchandise' than Ontario did because it relied on abundant supplies of semi-skilled labour, whereas Ontario's industry had been established and sustained by skilled immigrant German cabinet-makers. New types of postwar production and trade presented a welcome opportunity for Quebec designers and manufacturers to improve their relative situation.

Canada's first national industrial design competition was held in 1951, sponsored by the National Industrial Design Committee. Entrants were simply asked to 'design products for the house or garden.'[11] Five winners, selected from 330 entries, were each awarded $500. Julien Hébert, of the l'École des Beaux Arts in Montreal, was one winner, for an aluminum-tube and canvas garden chair (a triangular version of the Hardoy 'butterfly' chair of the 1930s). Another prize-winner, Pierre Gauvin, of Quebec, submitted a design for a metal-frame lounge chair with an expanded metal seat. James Warren, of the Ontario College of Art, won two prizes: one for drawings of a bent-plywood lounge chair on a tube base, and another for a prototype of a bent-plywood coffee table. The fifth award went to George Robb, of the University of Toronto School of Architecture, for a hanging metal light fixture.

The second competition, in 1952, had four official categories: Class A Wood (chairs for homes suitable for 'production and marketing of at least five thousand' units per year), Class B Aluminum (chairs for 'homes, gardens, restaurants or offices,'

Fig. 148 Design class at l'École du Meuble, Montreal, December 1953. In foreground, Father A. LeContey instructs fourth-year student P. Deschenaux (Chris Lund/National Film Board of Canada/National Archives of Canada/PA-183069)

five thousand units per year), Class C Wood (desks for homes, suitable for production and marketing of at least one hundred units per year), Class D Aluminum (door hardware). The judges were George Nelson, the American architect, industrial designer, and critic; G. Allan Burton, general manager of the Robert Simpson Company; Professor E.A. Allcut, head of the University of Toronto School of Engineering; J.S. Luck, designer at Aluminum Laboratories, in Kingston, Ontario; and architect John B. Parkin, president of the Association of Canadian Industrial Designers. One of these judges was quoted anonymously by *Canadian Homes and Gardens* as saying there was 'a defnite improvement' over the previous year's efforts, and that Canadian design was 'looking up.' The top prize, a generous $1,000, went to Laurie McIntosh, of Toronto, for a moulded-plywood and steel-tube desk chair, entered in Class A Wood, which was displayed with a prize-winning desk by Frank Dudas, also of Toronto (fig. 149). Hugh Dodds, of Oakville, won $250 for a plywood stacking chair. Another prize went to Charles Blais, of Winnipeg, for a pedestal desk. Domestic architecture was more energetically modern in the Prairie and Western provinces than elsewhere in Canada. Progressive architectural firms experimented with the new organicism in interior design, often using large expanses of glazing, natural wood or stone walls, wooden floors, pale colours, and blond-wood furniture. One of the most prominent of these award-winning firms was Semmens and Simpson, in Vancouver, a partnership including Douglas Simpson, who was co-designer of the National Research Council moulded-plastic chair.

In British Columbia, the fabrics selected for upholstery and drapery were often plain, so as not to compete for attention with the views and lush vegetation outside. Larger, open-plan spaces allowed for more expansive living-room furniture (fig. 150), and the milder West Coast climate required a less rigid demarcation between indoors and out, encouraging a more adventurous use of lightweight, multipurpose furniture.

Many designs of this type were made by Perpetua Furniture, in the South Granville district of Vancouver, established by Peter Cotton and his partner, Alfred Staples, in 1951. Cotton had been actively involved in the setting-up of the School of Architecture at the University of British Columbia, which he attended between 1947 and 1955.[12] The modest wood and wrought-iron chairs and tables he designed for Perpetua (figs.151–4) appealed to the retail buying public as well as to architects. Many of Cotton's designs were included in the 'Design Index' and were sold in central Canada by Morgan's department stores.

Earle Morrison and Robin Bush started designing furniture together in 1950, working out of a factory that Morrison acquired from Standard Furniture, in Victoria. He had studied aeronautical engineering at the California Institute of Technology and worked briefly in the plywood-components section of Hughes Aircraft.[13] Bush had studied art and design at the Vancouver School of Art. Their furniture quickly became popular, winning many National Industrial Design Council awards. It was sold locally by Standard Furniture, and across the country by Eaton's. Most of the Morrison Bush furniture was equally adaptable to commercial and residential interiors (figs.155–9), and Bush established his own company,

Fig. 149 Chair: moulded plywood, solid wood, steel tube. Designed by Lawrie McIntosh, Toronto. Winner of Best Design award, second national product-design competition, 1952. Desk: solid wood, steel tube. Designed by Frank Dudas, Toronto (*Canadian Homes and Gardens*, April 1952)

Fig. 150 Contour chair and stool: metal, bent laminated wood, upholstery. Designed by Strahan and Sturhan, Architects, Vancouver, *ca* 1953 (*West Coast Modern Furniture, 1945–60* catalogue, Vancouver Art Gallery, 1988. Photo: Jim Jardine, Vancouver Art Gallery)

Fig. 151 Dining chair: moulded plywood, steel rod.
Designed by Peter Cotton, Vancouver, 1951. Manufactured
by Perpetua Furniture, Vancouver (Photo: Graham Warrington,
Provincial Archives of British Columbia/98303-40)

Fig. 152 Dining chair: moulded plywood, steel rod,
upholstery. Designed by Peter Cotton, 1951. Manufactured
by Perpetua Furniture, Vancouver (*The Design Index*,
published by the National Gallery of Canada, Ottawa 1951)

Fig. 153 Coffee table: steel rod, steel sections, cast-wired glass. Designed by Peter Cotton, 1950. Manufactured by Perpetua Furniture, Vancouver (*The Design Index*, published by the National Gallery of Canada, Ottawa 1951)

Fig. 154 Lounge chair: steel rod, steel sections, flat steel, upholstery. Designed by Peter Cotton, *ca* 1951 (Photo: Graham Warrington, Provincial Archives of British Columbia/HP98006)

Fig. 155 Reception area in advertising agency, Cockfield Brown & Company, Vancouver. Seating designed by Robin Bush and Earle Morrison. Coffee table and ashtray designed by Peter Cotton. Mural by Jack Shadbolt (*Royal Architectural Institute of Canada Journal,* May 1955)

Fig. 156 Dining room in residence of architect D.C. Simpson, Vancouver. Chairs in steel rod, bent laminated wood, upholstery. Table in steel rod and laminated wood. Designed by Earle Morrison (Robin Bush Associates catalogue)

Fig. 157 Chair: bent laminated wood, woven paper cord. Designed by Earle Morrison and Robin Bush (Robin Bush Associates catalogue)

Fig. 158 Lounge chair: steel rod, solid wood, upholstery.
Designed by Earle Morrison and Robin Bush, Vancouver,
1951 (Robin Bush Associates catalogue)

Fig. 159 Sofa: solid wood, upholstery. Designed by Earle
Morrison and Robin Bush, Vancouver, 1951 (Robin Bush
Associates catalogue)

Robin Bush Associates Ltd, with offices in Vancouver and Toronto, to take contract orders from architects and interior designers. The new company presented work by Bush, Cotton, and Morrison, who remained an associate of the firm. He manufactured their designs, as well as Herman Miller products under licence, for the West Coast market. Morrison later opened his own design office in Vancouver, and spent a year at Knoll Furniture, in New York, working on furniture and interior designs for the B.C. Electric Building in Vancouver.

In Winnipeg, much of the design work was done by graduates and faculty of the School of Architecture at the University of Manitoba. A team of three people from the school, J.A. McCuish, Hugh McMillan, and Hugh McMillan, submitted a folding dining table to the 1951 national design competition, and, although the table didn't win a prize, a photograph of it was published in *Canadian Homes and Gardens*.[14]

Architect A.J. Donahue, co-designer of the National Research Council moulded-plastic chair, had an architectural practice in Winnipeg, in which he continued to design furniture, and taught at the University of Manitoba (fig. 160). The university was a magnet for students interested in interior design, as the degree program offered through its School of Architecture was the only one of its kind in the country. In other provinces, interior design was taught through diploma programs at art schools and technical colleges.

Imperial Furniture (previously Imperial Rattan), in Stratford, Ontario, advertised in 1950 for a professional wood-furniture designer. A young Dutch designer, Jan Kuypers, who was then working in Scotland, saw the advertisement in a British trade publication and successfully applied for the position. He was the son of a furniture maker and had studied furniture design at the Academy of Art and Architecture in the Hague. While working in Glasgow, Kuypers won first prize in a competition sponsored by the Scottish Manufacturers' Association. Moving to Stratford in early 1951, Kuypers arrived with thorough professional training, and typical Dutch sensitivity to appropriateness of design, especially in regard to scale (fig. 161). By July of that year, he had been appointed Imperial's chief designer.

Kuypers's transformation of the company's products enabled Imperial to compete successfully with Scandinavian furniture and with 'Scandinavian-style' lines from the United States. His designs, all executed in birch, introduced a precise, efficient minimalism previously absent from Canadian furniture manufacturing, and many enjoyed unprecedented levels of sales in both the retail and the contract markets (figs. 162–4).

Canada's fledgling community of industrial designers struggled to do significant work. Some were hired as consultants by the small number of firms willing to pay for professional design. Others set up their own entrepreneurial initiatives, relying on the services of small fabrication companies and independent retailers. Many of the successful experiments of the early 1950s were modest exercises in wrought iron, a material eminently suitable for small-scale experimentation and contract fabrication (figs. 165–8).

Fig. 160 Lounge chair: bent plywood, steel tube, uphol-
stery. Designed by A.J. Donahue, Winnipeg, *ca* 1954.
(Photo: Sheila Spence and Ernest Mayer, Winnipeg Art
Gallery, 1992)

Fig. 161 Dining or desk chair: yellow birch with baked-resin
finish, moulded plywood, upholstery. Designed by Jan
Kuypers, 1953. Manufactured by Imperial Furniture, Stratford
(*Design Awards 1953*, National Industrial Design Council,
Ottawa)

Fig. 162 Chest of drawers with mirror: yellow birch. Designed by Jan Kuypers. Manufactured by Imperial Furniture, Stratford (*The Design Index*, National Industrial Design Council, Ottawa, 1953)

Fig. 163 Lounge chair: yellow birch, upholstery. Designed by Jan Kuypers, 1953. Manufactured by Imperial Furniture, Stratford (*The Design Index*, National Industrial Design Council, Ottawa, 1953)

Fig. 164 Sofa manufactured by Imperial Furniture, Stratford, 1964 (National Archives of Canada/PA-183159)

Fig. 165 Chair: wrought iron, cane. Designed by Court Noxon, Toronto. Manufactured by Metalsmiths (*The Design Index*, National Industrial Design Council, Ottawa, 1953)

Fig. 166 Lounge chair: wrought iron, expanded metal, upholstery. Designed by George Boake, Toronto. Manufactured by Metalsmiths (*Design Awards 1953*, National Industrial Design Council, Ottawa)

Fig. 167 The 'Video' chair: wrought iron, bent plywood, upholstery. Manufactured by Arrow Bedding (Eastern) Limited, Toronto (*Furniture and Furnishings*, Toronto, April 1954)

Fig. 168 Chair: wrought iron, wicker. Designed by Charles Szucsany, Montreal, 1954 (*Canadian Homes and Gardens*, July 1954)

The early work of Montreal designer Jacques Guillon illustrates the *ad hoc* nature of the process. Guillon, who had studied architecture at McGill University, designed a chair that could be used as a dining chair or side chair, composed of a laminated-wood frame, perforated and woven with nylon cord (fig. 169). Initial production was handled by Andreef, a Montreal manufacturer of laminated, woven tennis racquets and laminated-wood skis (fig. 170). Some people were so impressed by published photographs of the Guillon dining chair that they made the long drive from Toronto to Montreal to buy it at Pego's, the furnishings store run by Guillon's wife, Pego Mc-Naughton. Guillon's woven chair design was a significant contribution to modernism's distinguished array of 'small, capricious chairs.'[15]

The extremely low level of funding for the art and design activities of the National Gallery of Canada was revealed in the spring of 1951, when a report was issued by the Royal Commission on National Development in the Arts, Letters, and Sciences (the Massey Commission). The gallery's annual appropriation from Parliament could not bear comparison with the budgets of major regional galleries in the United States, and the gallery, therefore, could not meet the expectations of the art community in its purchases of Canadian and foreign art. It also could not meet the expectations of smaller cities wanting to have travelling art and design exhibitions from the gallery's temporary and permanent collections. The royal commission recommended substantially increased funding for all the National Gallery's programs.

It also recommended the establishment of a 'government-supported body' to be known as the Canada Council. This council would encourage the 'Arts, Letters, Humanities and Social Sciences' to 'stimulate and to help voluntary organisations within these fields,' and to 'foster Canada's cultural relations abroad.' The council would administer a system of grants for 'persons engaged in the arts and letters for work and study either in Canada or abroad' as well as grants for people from other countries to study in Canada. In its comments on the state of the country's architecture and town planning, the commission noted that it had 'received disturbing reports.' Architecture was said to be 'ignored by the public,' who had 'little respect for the past,' and were 'heedless about the future' and 'apathetic or confused about the present.' The state of design, whether industrial or craft, was not mentioned.

The National Gallery, however, continued to be active in the organizing of travelling design exhibitions. One of these, 'Industrial Design, 1951 BC–AD 1951,' opened at the Royal Ontario Museum in January 1951 and was later shown in Ottawa, Winnipeg, and Calgary. The exhibition featured the familiar didactic panels, including one with a large, watchful eye floating over the motto 'Canadian Industrial Design Needs You.' These panels were mounted on display stands designed by the Toronto architect George Englesmith. The groups of contemporary and historical furniture in the exhibition included work by Eames, Breuer, Thonet, and Englesmith himself. His somewhat ungainly chair was later published in the British magazine *Design* with the caption: 'Canadian contribution to the steel-tube-and-bent-plywood school of furniture design: the Englechair ...'[16]

Fig. 169 Chair: laminated wood with black lacquer, white nylon cord (also available in natural maple or walnut, and with brown nylon cord). Designed by Jacques Guillon, Montreal, 1950. Manufactured by Modernart, Montreal (*The Design Index*, National Industrial Design Council, Ottawa, 1953)

Fig. 170 Advertisement for Andreef Chairs, Montreal. Advertisement designed by Jean Fortin (*Toronto Art Directors' Club Annual*, 1953)

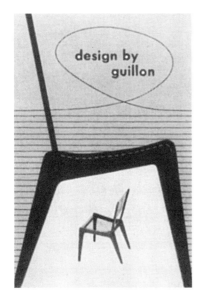

Fig. 171 Two Vancouver designers showing their prize-winning chairs to the prime minister at opening of exhibition, Design Merit Awards to Industry, April 1953. Left to right: designer Alfred Staples, Prime Minister Louis St-Laurent, designer Peter Cotton, and Minister of Trade and Commerce C.D. Howe *(Design [U.K.],* no. 56, 1953)

Fig. 172 Display at the Design Centre, Ottawa, November
1953, comparing 1950s living room with 1920s sitting room.
Furniture by Jacques Guillon, Jan Kuypers, and others
(National Film Board, National Archives of Canada/PA-183068)

Furniture by Guillon, Kuypers, Cotton, Bush, Morrison, and others was displayed at the first government-sponsored Design Centre, opened in Ottawa in April 1953 by Prime Minister Louis St-Laurent (fig. 171). The Design Centre, on the ground floor of the Laurentian Building, was managed by the National Gallery. Its construction costs of $53,000 had been paid by the Department of Public Works. The gallery paid for the upkeep of the centre, staff salaries, and most of the cost of exhibitions, out of its regular appropriations from Parliament. The Design Centre included a small gallery space and counter where the public could purchase reproductions of paintings from the National Gallery and other Canadian art museums. There was also a reading room, with product catalogues and magazines, as well as offices and storage rooms.

The centre's principal exhibition space was quite modest. Furniture was placed directly on the floor, some in life-like groupings (fig. 172). There was often a sprinkling of didactic panels on walls and partitions. The appearance of the centre suggests that its operating costs were kept to a minimum, and the low-key atmosphere certainly emphasized Buchanan's slogan that these were 'Canadian designs for everyday use.'

Humphrey Carver, chairman of the Research Committee at the Central Mortgage and Housing Corporation (CMHC), in Ottawa, wrote a report for *Canadian Art* on the centre's first year of operation.[17] He praised the range of exhibitions that had been shown. These included a study of furniture design for small homes prepared in collaboration with CMHC, a photographic exhibition of contemporary Italian architecture, and a Christmas display of gifts for under $15 from Ottawa shops. The last was so successful that the shops sold out of those products well before Christmas Day. The Design Centre, according to Carver, had 'struck a new note,' bringing design away from the 'institutions of mausoleum character' and 'into Main Street.'

In his speech opening the Design Centre, the prime minister had announced the inauguration of annual Design Merit Awards for industrial products. The institution of these annual awards, he said, 'will have a beneficial effect on Canadian industry in years to come in terms of more attractive and saleable products both in domestic and foreign markets. Moreover, the consumers among whom all Canadians are numbered will benefit. They will be able to obtain goods which are more efficient in function, more pleasing to the eye, and more appealing to the purse.'[18] The awards were sponsored and judged by the National Industrial Design Council, which at this time consisted of twenty members representing 'manufacturers, retailers, consumers, designers, research workers, educationists and members of ... government agencies interested in design and production for home and export.' To be eligible, products had to be made, but not necessarily designed, in Canada. In the first year, however, thirty-seven of the forty-six winning products announced at the new Design Centre were the work of Canadian designers. Jan Kuypers was spectacularly successful, winning twenty-five Design Awards for Imperial in the first three years of the award program, from 1953 to 1955.

In 1955, Alan Jarvis was appointed director of the National Gallery. Jarvis, a Canadian, had been a well-known spokesman for design in England through his work as the first public-relations officer for the British Council of Industrial Design. The enthusiasm of Ottawa design advocates, however, apparently did not extend beyond exhibitions and publishing into the realm of collecting. The National Gallery tentatively began to acquire a furniture collection during the 1950s, possibly choosing to hang onto the best pieces from the 'Design Index' and the Design Centre for future display. But this Canadian furniture collection – the only one of its kind ever initiated – was not officially announced or endowed, and was eventually neglected, forgotten, and dispersed.

Fig. 173 Canadian display at the Milan Triennale, 1954. Woven chair, at left, by Morrison-Bush; cabinet and lounge chair by Jan Kuypers; magazine rack by Jacques Guillon; tripod lamp by Peter Cotton; desk by Frank Dudas; desk chair by Lawrie McIntosh (*Canadian Art*, New Year 1955)

Design Issues

Canada participated in the Milan Triennale for the first time in 1954. This was the tenth *triennale*, an international exposition of contemporary architecture and design. The modest Canadian installation (fig. 173) consisted of a living/dining room with small adjoining kitchen. It was furnished with award-winning pieces from the 'Design Index.' A writer in the Swedish magazine *Form* praised the Canadian and Dutch displays at the *triennale* for their 'sobriety,' while somewhat ungraciously criticizing the design 'eccentricity' of their hosts, the Italians.[1] Canada returned to Milan for the 1957 *triennale* with an installation that featured an interior-design project by Robin Bush, commissioned for miners' housing in Kitimat, British Columbia. *Canadian Art* reported that the Canadian display was the only one in Milan with 'a social theme.' It was later claimed by Norman Hay, in a 1958 article in *Canadian Art*, that the Milanese display of Bush's furniture and interior design for workers' housing caused a significant increase in immigration to Canada by working-class Italians, although Canadian government policy at the time officially favoured immigration by 'professional people.'

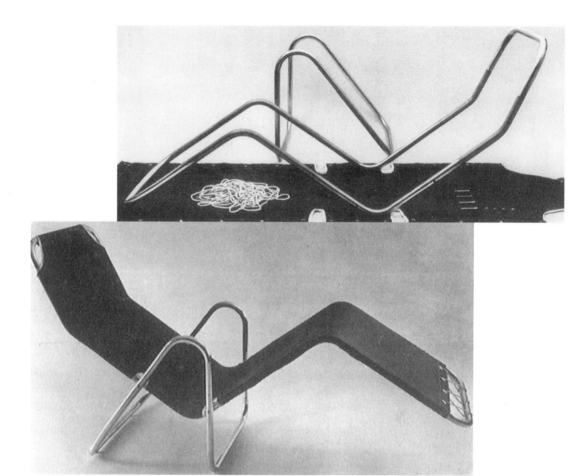

Fig. 174 (a) Garden chaise-longue frame and cover: aluminum tube, canvas. Designed by Julien Hébert, Montreal (*Domus*, Milan, November 1954); (b) Garden chaise-longue, aluminum tube, canvas. Designed by Julien Hébert. Manufactured by Siegmund Werner, Montreal (*Decorative Art* annual, Studio Publications, London, 1954–5)

Fig. 175 (a) Chair frame and cover: aluminum tube, canvas. Designed by Julien Hébert, Montreal (*Domus*, Milan, November 1954); (b) Chair: aluminum tube, canvas (red, green, blue, or orange). Designed by Julien Hébert, Montreal. Manufactured by Siegmund Werner Ltd, Montreal (*The Design Index*, National Industrial Design Council, Ottawa, 1953)

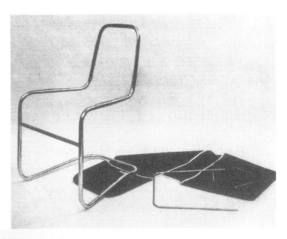

Canada's display at the 1954 *triennale* included a chaise-longue and a chair (figs. 174 and 175) by Montreal designer Julien Hébert, who had been one of the five winners in the country's first industrial design competition in 1951. Hébert exploited the cool minimalism of aluminum in his garden-furniture designs for the Siegmund Werner Company, of Montreal (fig. 176). The pieces sent to Milan were published in English and Italian design magazines, and were shown again in an exhibition sponsored by Alcan, which Hébert organized for the National Industrial Design Council in 1956.

This exhibition was an important survey of contemporary design in aluminum, reported by the New York magazine *Industrial Design* to be circulating among museums and art galleries in a number of American cities (fig. 177). It included twenty products designed and made in Canada, as well as approximately sixty other products from the United States, the United Kingdom, Belgium, Denmark, Finland, France, Germany, Italy, Japan, Norway, Sweden, and Switzerland. The only furniture in the aluminum exhibition, apart from Hébert's chaise-longue, were two chairs from Switzerland, by Hans Coray; a roll-top desk by George Nelson and a chair by David Weinstock, both American; and a dining chair from England, by Ernest Race.

Canadian commentators reported on the more radical experiments of European design with the same lack of enthusiasm they had demonstrated in the 1920s. For example, the 1955 edition of an important series of Italian decorative arts books, *L'Arredamento Moderno*, was reviewed in the *RAIC Journal* by Toronto architect William Grierson. Grierson described the international glass and ceramic work in *L'Arredamento Moderno* as 'weird' and 'useless,' and said that none of the fabrics illustrated would be 'of any interest to an Architect.' The energetic eclecticism of the work was apparently too highly charged for Grierson's low-key Canadian taste. 'This book,' he concluded, 'makes painfully clear the artistic chaos in the world today. It seems we have a long way to go to achieve that beautiful and consistent expression which has been evident in previous and more tranquil societies.' Grierson did not indicate which previous tranquil societies he had in mind.

Canadian shoppers had the opportunity to see new furniture from all over the country in national magazines (plate 7) and urban retail stores. One could see furniture by Peter Cotton of Vancouver at Morgan's department stores in Montreal, Ottawa, and Toronto, while Russell Spanner's designs were sold at Morgan's and Simpson's, and at Eaton's stores 'from coast to coast.' Eaton's became a truly national chain in 1955, when the company opened a store in Charlottetown, Prince Edward Island. In 1956 the company made its first move into a regional shopping centre, in Oshawa, Ontario.

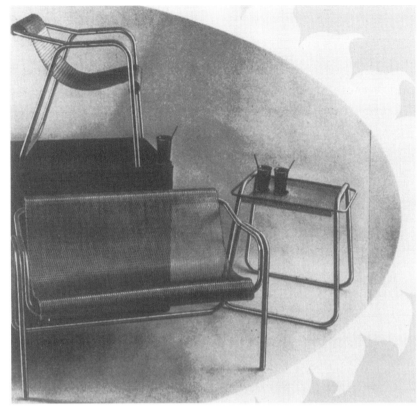

Fig. 176 Garden furniture: aluminum tube, aluminum mesh.
Designed by Julien Hébert, Montreal. Manufactured by Siegmund Werner, Montreal (*Furniture and Furnishings*, 1953)

Fig. 177 'Design in Aluminum' exhibition sponsored by
Alcan, curated by Julien Hébert (*Industrial Design*, New
York, February 1956)

Fig. 178 Stool: walnut and woven cord. Designed by John Stene, Toronto, 1958. Made by Brunswick Manufacturing (Photo: Sheila Spence and Ernest Mayer, Winnipeg Art Gallery, 1992)

Fig. 179 Table: walnut. Designed by John Stene, Toronto, *ca* 1957. Made by Brunswick Manufacturing, Toronto (National Archives of Canada/NL-17918)

At stores in major cities one could also see unusual imported furniture, such as wrought-iron garden chairs from Italy, or bentwood chairs and tables by Swedish designer Bruno Mathsson. In 1951, Morgan's featured glamorous cork-topped mahogany tables and cabinets by American designer Paul Frankl, while Eaton's later advertised plywood furniture by Charles Eames and by Finn Juhl. These pieces were described as being cheap enough and light enough to be moved around from 'urban recreation rooms' in the winter to country cottages in the summer.

The biggest retail design promotion of the 1950s was the Trend House. This was a series of full-scale model homes built in Toronto, Halifax, London, Winnipeg, Regina, Edmonton, Vancouver, and Victoria. Sponsored by the British Columbia Lumber Manufacturers' Association, and furnished by Eaton's, these houses displayed the latest in Canadian furniture, textiles, craft, and appliances. The designers of the Toronto Trend House were the architects Fleury, Arthur, and Calvert. Bob Calvert, a graduate of the School of Architecture at the University of Toronto, was the designer whose webbed, assemble-yourself, plywood lounge chair had been featured at the 'Design for Living' exhibition in Vancouver in 1949.[2] And Eric Arthur had been the editor of the RAIC Journal at the time of its special 'Design in Industry' issue in 1947.

Many of the products displayed inside and outside the Trend Houses were from the 'Design Index.' These could also be seen in model homes and model rooms at the annual Canadian National Exhibition in Toronto, which provided a particularly good opportunity to catch the attention of young couples and families on the look-out for new products and decorating ideas.

The department stores, however, began to neglect the interior and merchandising design of their own retailing premises, although they continued to stress the value of modern design in store advertising and promotion. A different type of display – more casual, less substantial – was seen to be the right way to show most products in new suburban malls. By the early 1960s, the department stores had abandoned their role as design trend-setters, no longer attempting to inspire customers through the lavishness or fashionable stylishness of 'the setting.' The display of home furnishings returned to pre-1928 standards, with merchandise lined up in rows to maximize inventory. Most of the furniture displayed, and sold, was traditional in style. As one retailer later observed, 'modern' was 'a dirty word in the Canadian furniture business.'[3]

Design journalism was, for a brief period, equally unhelpful to conscientious designers and consumers. In 1956, Patricia Lamont, Home Planning Editor of Canadian Homes and Gardens, wrote a report on that year's furniture trade shows in Chicago and Toronto. Her report did not include the names of any designers, manufacturers, or retailers. Key phrases, printed in bold type, were reminiscent of the vague wisps of description popular in the 1930s: 'more pattern,' 'lighter shades,' 'dull lustre.' The only name mentioned was that of Patricia Lamont (twice), and the accompanying solitary photograph was not of a piece of furniture, or a designer, or even a trade show; it was a portrait of Patricia Lamont.

Scandinavian imports gradually became the furnishings of choice for affluent homes across the country. In Montreal, Pego's sold Scandinavian furniture and accessories in addition to their Canadian designs. Shelagh's in Toronto, started in the early 1950s by John and Shelagh Stene, was the best known of the Scandinavian suppliers, selling a wide range of furniture from Denmark, Sweden, and Finland. Stene, a Norwegian engineer, later set up Brunswick Manufacturing, to produce his own designs (figs.178 and 179). Larry Henderson established an importing company, Scantrade, to market and distribute Scandinavian products, and in 1958 the venerable Danish firm George Jensen opened a three-storey shop on Bloor Street in Toronto. A report on the opening of the Jensen store in *The Canadian Architect* noted that the refined intimacy of the store's displays suggested to the shopper that 'you are already in possession of what you see.'

Art, craft, and design were presented together in stores and galleries throughout the 1950s. Retail displays and design exhibitions in galleries usually included handmade and machine-made objects as well as art and photography. This egalitarian approach was demonstrated in 1959, when the Vancouver Art Gallery hosted a juried crafts show and one of the fine craft awards was sponsored by the British Columbia Industrial Design Committee. Many National Industrial Design Council Awards were given for craft design, most notably the superb upholstery fabrics by weaver and Royal Ontario Museum curator Harold Burnham.

One of the first programs shown on Canadian television, in September 1952, was a series called *Design in Living*, written and narrated by the Canadian painter Arthur Lismer.[4] Several well-known designers and design advocates, such as Julien Hébert, who later served as chairman of the Canada Council, were trained as artists, and public art galleries continued to host design exhibitions. Designers and craftspeople borrowed from, and contributed to, the work of artists in a continually replenishing cycle of experimentation and appropriation. Textile manufacturers, for example, borrowed freely from craft weavers for textural innovation, and from graphic designers and artists for imagery and colours. Articles and photo surveys in mass-market magazines and art journals eagerly mixed and matched art and design. Room settings always included paintings, usually abstract, and accompanying close-up photos juxtaposed craft or design objects with details of paintings or sculpture. These 'artistic' groupings were meant to promote the appreciation of art and design but often tended to confuse, rather than clarify, the divergent interests of both.

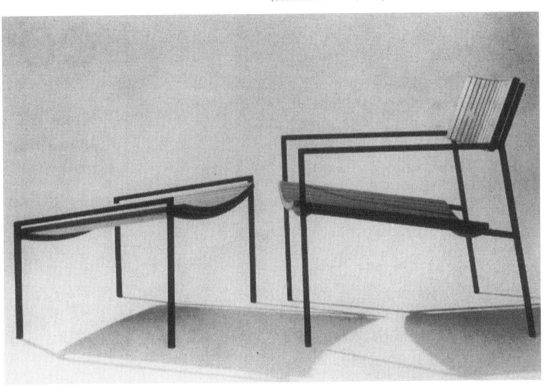

Fig. 180 Garden chair and stool: wrought iron, solid wood.
Designed by Court Noxon, Toronto, *ca* 1960. Manufactured
by Metalsmiths. Exhibited at Milan Triennale, 1963
(*Canadian Interiors*, 1964)

Fig. 181 Coffee table: birch. Manufactured by Snyder's,
Waterloo (Photo: William Deacon, Toronto, 1985)

Fig. 182 Dining chair and armchair: walnut, upholstery. Designed by Sigrun Bulow-Hube, Montreal, 1958 (*Canadian Homes and Gardens*, May 1958)

In 1954, John B. Parkin Associates won a design competition held by the Ontario Association of Architects, for a new building in Toronto to house the association's offices and meeting-rooms. A furnishing committee, composed of three architects – John C. Parkin, Gordon Adamson, and A.S. Mathers – selected all of the furnishings. The committee eschewed patriotism, looking at work from other countries as well as Canada, but announced that it had ended up being forced by 'economics' to buy Canadian 'wherever possible,' although Swedish armchairs and coffee tables were bought for the library, and Danish dining chairs for the members' lounge.[5] Aka Works in Montreal designed and made the boardroom chairs, but the furnishing-committee architects complained that, apart from these pieces, 'very little suitable Canadian-made furniture was to be found on the market.'

Presumably for this reason, all the other pieces of furniture in the building – desks, boardroom tables, coffee tables, benches, end tables, chesterfields, upholstered lounge chairs, dining tables, and lectern – were designed by the architects themselves.[6] They were designed to be 'supplementary to the architecture,' using subdued upholstery colours to match the natural materials of the walls and floors. In addition, the committee of architects felt that the furniture, already subordinated to the interior architecture, should further 'contain itself as a background to the individuals using the building.' The resulting room settings were restrained to the point of ordinariness, suggesting, as did the design of several domestic interiors by the Parkin office in the 1950s, that this distinguished modern architectural practice was somewhat lacking in furniture-design savvy.

Canadian furniture designers were supported in principle but dismissed in practice by Canadian architects. This rebuff was a serious blow to the newly emerging industrial design profession, already a decade or more behind the Americans in education, research, and development. Articles in popular and professional magazines sometimes showed architect-designed homes with Canadian furniture, but usually failed to mention the names of the designers or manufacturers. Magazines often required readers to write in for even the most basic information about designers and products, thereby building mailing lists for publishers and advertisers, but adversely affecting the ability of prospective customers to identify and obtain Canadian furniture and furnishings.

Canadian architectural journals published photographs of winning furniture designs from industrial design competitions and exhibitions, but the resulting products rarely appeared in reports on architectural projects shown in the same journals. The majority of architect-designed homes and offices in Canada, as in many other countries, were furnished with products from the Herman Miller Furniture Company and Knoll Furniture (plate 8). Frank Moritsugu, writer and editor for *Canadian Homes and Gardens*, reported in March 1955 that these two American companies were now having some of their products made in Canada, for the Canadian market. These included the 'womb chair' by Eero Saarinen (described by Moritsugu as the 'cuddle chair'), Charles Eames's moulded-ply and steel-tube chairs, and an upholstered chaise-longue by George Nelson. CB Wrought Iron Manufacturing Company, in Toronto, later known as CB Metals, manufactured two lines of steel furniture for Knoll, designed by Harry Bertoia and Warren Platner.

Equally high standards of fabrication were available at other local companies such as Metalsmiths, the firm founded by Kenneth Noxon and now run by his son, Court, a 1953 graduate of the University of Toronto School of Architecture. Court Noxon continued the use of wrought iron, his father's material of choice, but also used flat steel and steel tube, as well as wood and woven cane (fig. 180). Several of his designs won National Industrial Design Council Awards, most notably a wall-mounted, infinitely extendable, steel and wood coat-and-hat-rack system, still in production in the 1990s. Noxon's sophisticated designs for fireplace equipment continued another tradition of the firm, as his father's earliest advertised products were fire-screens, including one with a large spider in a radiating web. Metalsmiths' modus operandi shifted over the years from an entirely craft-based method of production to a combination of industrial processes and handwork.

A furniture conference, the first in Canada, was organized in 1955 by the National Industrial Design Council. Held in Toronto, it was attended by more than a hundred manufacturers, retailers, and designers. The speeches given at the conference and the 'lively discussion which followed' were published by the council, and excerpts were printed in *Canadian Art* under the heading 'Do Canadians Want Modern Furniture?' George Soulis, staff designer for Snyder's (fig. 181), pointed out that labour costs were the most important consideration in the development of a new design for production. In 1930 Snyder's had been making chairs that required 112 hours of labour, and sold for $35. This was obviously no longer possible.

W.A.D. Murray, merchandise manager of Henry Morgan and Company, analysed his store's contradictory sales figures. A large majority of the customers for dining-room suites (82 per cent) bought traditional designs, while the majority of bedroom-suite customers (66 per cent) chose modern designs. Murray thought that the solution to this puzzle lay in the fact that 'the bedroom is apart from other rooms ... behind closed doors' (where one presumably could act out one's shameless modern fantasies). Bedrooms also contained few if any inherited items, and rarely had to accommodate 'awkward wedding gifts.' The dining room, on the other hand, often had to show off traditional china and silverware designs. The dining room also often had a 'doorless' connection to a traditionally furnished living room, and had to be 'part of the general décor.'[7]

The designer Robin Bush declared in his speech at the conference that modern furniture would find customers 'anywhere in the world' if sufficient attention was paid to controlling manufacturing costs. He thought that Canadian design was 'more poorly advertised and presented by all companies concerned than in any other country.' The directors of manufacturing and retailing companies, if they were going into the field of modern design, had to pay attention to 'their letterheads, the painting of their trucks, and the way their president ties his tie.' Bush encouraged his listeners to abandon calls for 'indigenous Canadian design.' Good design was international and 'affected by the economic, the architectural, the political and other changes going on around us.' He called on Canadian architects to start building better modern buildings that would stimulate interest in modern furniture.

Fig. 183 Armchair: steel rod, turned walnut, canvas webbing, upholstery. Designed by Robert Kaiser, Toronto, 1956 (*Decorative Art* annual, Studio Publications, London, 1957–8)

Fig. 184 Armchairs by Robert Kaiser. Kaiser residence, Toronto (*Canadian Homes and Gardens*, August 1958)

Bush's worldly-wise advice contrasted sharply with the homely observations made by Mr Murray from Morgan's, who explored, in peculiar detail, the question of gender in relation to furniture sales:

> The customer is a woman. She is the chatelaine, she is the drudge, she is the provider of taste. It is she who entertains, it is she who dresses her background as a foil to her beauty. Today more than ever she is also working at a career, getting married young and planning a bigger family than she came from. Her modern kitchen is the keynote to her thinking.
>
> Then where is mere man in this picture? He is less interested in the home than in the car, the hockey match, the garden, the office. He is the keeper of the purse. He it is who, more often than not, prevents the fulfillment of the decorator's dream. He it is that reclines in the monstrous chair that defies any tasteful scheme to hide and that no wife or maid can move without his help.
>
> Why then bother with the male? Alas, he is the keeper of the purse, and if we are going to do an educational job we must start on the schoolteacher who reaches the boy, the professor who expands the youthful mind. The journal that *pater familias* tends to read must be reached and the television set he absorbs must be used if we are to bring home to father his responsibilities to his family in matters of taste.

Most retail customers and magazine readers were women, as were many of the country's retailers, designers, and journalists. Women were also significant leaders of the various regional crafts communities. But, in the business of making and selling production furniture, they were largely limited to their roles in advertisements, as glamorous career girls or harried housewives, constantly in need of new styles and new products. In the mid-1950s *Canadian Homes and Gardens* had a regular, small column called 'What the Women Want.' It was an advice column limited to practical information about household chores and appliances.

In 1959 the journalist Margit Bennett began writing for *Canadian Homes and Gardens*. As a reporter and editor, Bennett became an influential advocate of Canadian design. Her writing was reliably informative, graciously mixing Canadian products and imported goods without drawing undue attention to the geographic origins of either. Her sophisticated choice of editorial material and enthusiastic support for designers brought Canadian decorative-arts reporting back to the conscientious days of Mary-Etta Macpherson in the 1920s. Bennett was later manager of a government-sponsored Design Centre in Toronto.

The journalist Robert Fulford wrote an article for *Canadian Homes and Gardens* in 1958 titled 'What Is a Designer Anyway? And Why Is He Fighting in Your Living Room?' Fulford ploughed a familiar editorial furrow – 'What is design?' – and gave his own brief history of the field. He cited the Englishman William Morris as the first person to address the conflicts of art and industry, but criticized Morris's rejection of mass production. Fulford then contrasted the craft and art skills of Morris and his colleagues with the industrial design activities of the German Bauhaus, apparently overlooking both the impressive scale of Morris's manufacturing and retailing operations and the modest craft and art foundations of the Bauhaus.

Having set up this artificial conflict between craft history and design history, Fulford then used it to bolster his conclusion that the contemporary furniture designer was 'the product of a nervous marriage between machinery and art, comfort and beauty.' The designer, according to Fulford, could approach his work functionally and hope that it turned out to be beautiful, or he could 'begin with a series of lovely lines' and hope that they might make a comfortable chair.

By adding that Canadian designers should strive to be 'specifically Canadian in some way,' Fulford summarized with unselfconscious clarity the three most common misconceptions about modern industrial design: that it could, and should, attempt to formally convey idealized, nationalist characteristics; that it must, by its very nature, be in permanent, contentious conflict with both art and craft; and that it is, at all times, the declared enemy of domestic comfort and simple delight.[8]

The designers themselves did little to elevate or animate public discussion of furniture design. When a number of young designers were photographed in their own homes for a feature article in *Canadian Homes and Gardens* in 1958, all were quoted making fuzzy comments about their work. Jan Kuypers, for example, observed that 'a living room should be used for living,' while Court Noxon noted that 'furniture should be designed for people.'[9]

One of the designers featured in this article was Sigrun Bulow-Hube, who was quoted as saying that furniture should be 'casual but timeless.' Bulow-Hube had studied in Germany and Denmark, and had worked in Sweden, and then in the United States on a research scholarship. She immigrated to Canada in 1950 and started her own design firm in Montreal in 1953, subsequently winning many National Industrial Design Council Awards (fig. 182). Bulow-Hube, who designed furniture for Aka Works in Montreal, usually used oil-finished woods in the Scandinavian manner, and her chairs were often upholstered with fabrics from the studio of weaver Karen Bulow, who acted as craftsperson and textile consultant for several generations of Montreal designers.

The most unusual work shown in this 'young designers' issue of *Canadian Homes and Gardens* was that of Robert Kaiser, a freelance designer from Detroit who had settled in Toronto. His lounge-chair and dining-chair designs both used innovative combinations of steel rod and turned wood (figs. 183 and 184). They were finely scaled and well finished, taking maximum advantage of the rich, organic

Fig. 185 Dining chair: turned walnut, steel rod, upholstery.
Designed by Robert Kaiser, Toronto (*The Arts in Canada*, edited
by Malcolm Ross, published by Macmillan, Toronto, 1958)

properties of the walnut, contrasted with the industrial coolness of the chrome-plated steel. Kaiser's lounge-chair was published in England in Studio Publications' *Decorative Arts Annual* of 1957. His dining chair appeared as the only piece of furniture in a 1958 book titled *The Arts in Canada: A Stocktaking at Mid-Century*, in an extemely brief industrial-design chapter which was an uninformative sermon on sensible good taste, the search for perfect form, the mystery of beauty, and the vision of far-sighted men (fig. 185).[10]

Fig. 186 View of Canada Pavilion at Brussels World's Fair, 1958. Chairs designed by Jan Kuypers (*Canadian Art*, Winter 1957)

In the Spotlight

Furniture designed by Jan Kuypers was featured in the Canada pavilion at the Brussels World's Fair in 1958 (fig. 186). The careful advance planning of the pavilion was evidence of a newly elevated design consciousness in Ottawa. The Government Exhibition Commission began work on the project in 1955, and its first act was to set up a special interdepartmental committee of senior civil servants to 'guide and review all aspects of the work.'[1] They decided on the general themes for twenty-three exhibits, each of which was then assigned its own advisory committee with representatives from 'private organisations, industry and government.' A story sequence and controlled traffic flow was established, in a 'maze-type plan,' and designers from the Exhibition Commission and private firms developed the initial design concepts for the displays.

The pavilion, according to Donald Buchanan, was neither as ostentatious as the Russians' nor as open-handed as the Americans', and befitted a middle power like Canada.[2] He thought that it was spoiled, however, by too many factual displays, with too many explanatory texts. His comment suggests that Buchanan had wearied of his own didactic methods. In an uncharacteristic burst of wit, he even observed that 'the appearance is gay but the content too chaste.' Overall he thought, in a more customary tone, that the pavilion was 'almost a success, but not quite.'

An impressive furniture exhibition titled 'Contemporary Furnishings for the Home' was shown in 1958 at the Art Gallery of Ontario (fig. 187). This sparse, elegant display in the Walker Court of the gallery included pieces by Italian designer Oswaldo Borsani, and the Americans Florence Knoll and George Nelson, among others. One visitor to the exhibition was Walter Nugent, of Oakville, Ontario, an ex–advertising executive who went home inspired to try his hand at furniture design. Through extensive trial-and-error research in his home workshop, Nugent developed a clever and original idea for chair construction (figs. 188 and 189). The system he devised consisted of a one-piece seat-and-back frame made from a piece of bent, sprung steel rod. This inner frame was covered with a canvas sleeve which supported two cut sections of foam rubber forming the back and seat cushioning, and these in turn were covered with a woollen sleeve. This easily constructed and assembled seat-with-self-supporting-back could then be attached to a wide variety of wood or metal exterior frames, forming individual armchairs, swivel desk chairs, stacking chairs, or multi-unit sofas. Nugent set up a manufacturing company in Oakville and presented his designs at the 1961 Furniture Mart in Toronto, where they met with immediate success.

Furniture designers and manufacturers across the country benefited from a series of public building projects organized by the federal Department of Transport during the late 1950s and early 1960s. New airport terminals were built in Montreal (fig. 190), Gander, Saint John, Edmonton, Winnipeg, Ottawa, and Toronto. Stanley White, a 1949 University of Toronto architecture graduate working for the department in Ottawa, was given responsibility for the interior-design and furnishings contracts for most of these projects. White, an enlightened civil servant, encouraged Canadian designers to submit their ideas for furniture and fixtures and, in some cases, facilitated the production of these designs by working closely with both designers and manufacturers. He specified only furniture made in Canada but took advantage of the availability of many American designs then being manufactured in Canada under licence, using tables and seating by Charles Eames, George Nelson, and Harry Bertoia to supplement the Canadian furniture and fixtures (figs. 191 and 192).

Stefan Siwinski was one of the designers whose work was selected for the Toronto airport. His first published design, in 1959, was a cheeky three-legged dining chair with a small round back (fig. 193). The flat steel seating he produced for the airport projects was more substantial, and became part of a line of high-quality steel furniture for commercial interiors (fig. 194). Although Siwinski ran a relatively small operation as designer, manufacturer (in collaboration with local fabricators), and marketer, he could produce significant quantities of furniture. Five hundred chairs were made in ten weeks for the airport project.[3] During the 1960s, Siwinski worked with moulded acrylics and Fibreglas, producing geometric pedestal chairs, transparent 'bubble' chairs, and large dining tables (fig. 195).

Fig. 187 'Contemporary Furnishings for the Home,' an international furniture exhibition at the Art Gallery of Ontario, April 1958 (*The Canadian Architect*, August 1958)

Fig. 188 Armchair: walnut, sprung-steel frame, upholstery. Designed by Walter Nugent, Oakville, Ontario, 1960 (pictured). Manufactured by Walter Nugent Designs Limited (*Canadian Homes and Gardens*, 1960)

NEW IDEA IN CHAIRS AT THE MART

Oakville's Walter Nugent designs a chair with a self-supporting back

MOST INTRIGUING EXHIBIT at the Canadian Furniture Mart was the chair shown here. Designed by a former advertising man, its basic principle is that the back and seat are a single steel frame formed only in the chair seat but ingeniously bent so that the back is self-supporting. This revolutionary concept increases the chair's flexibility and comfort. And on an oiled walnut frame, the "floating back" adds to the chair's airy, yielding look. The basic steel frame is first covered with a casing sleeve, then floats rubber (on the progressive views above), and appears into its upholstery. To replace or remove cover, you simply loosen four bolts and snaps. Chair costs $80; extra cover $30.

Forty-seven-year-old Walter Nugent's chair is his debut in the Canadian furniture market. Until about seven years ago, this Oakville, Ont., man worked in advertising. Then aptitude tests indicated he had engineering and design ability. He quit his job; studied up on furniture—both design and the business end—in Canada, Denmark and Italy. Now he has his own manufacturing setup, from which come his chairs. Among his designs are two and three-seater interprovincial on the same steel support back principle, they spring from one basic Nugent belief: never Canadians ought to be more comfortable. □

Fig. 189 Office with seating and tables designed by Walter Nugent. Manufactured by Walter Nugent Designs Limited, Oakville (Nugent catalogue)

Fig. 190 Dorval airport, Montreal, 1959. Interior design by Jacques Guillon and Associates, Montreal. Seating designed by Chris Sorensen, Montreal, manufactured by Ebena of Canada, Quebec (Canadian Architectural Archives, University of Calgary, Panda Collection/601134.5)

Fig. 191 Airport seating: steel tube, flat steel, upholstery. Designed by Robin Bush, Toronto, 1963. Manufactured by Canadian Office and School Furniture Limited, Preston, Ontario (*Canadian Interiors*, October 1968)

Fig. 192 Airport seating designed by Robin Bush for the Toronto International Airport, 1964 (Canadian Architectural Archives, University of Calgary, Panda Collection/64040-97)

Fig. 193 Chair: steel rod, bent laminated wood, vinyl. Designed by Stefan Siwinski, Toronto, 1959 (*The Canadian Architect*, September 1960)

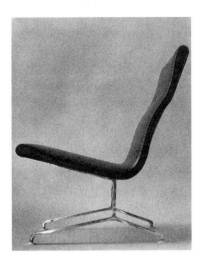

Fig. 194 Seating: chrome-plated flat steel, upholstery. Designed by Stefan Siwinski for the Toronto International Airport, 1964 (Ronald E. Vickers//National Archives of Canada/PA-183161)

Fig. 195 Armchair: moulded plastic. Designed and manufactured by Stefan Siwinski, Toronto (*Canadian Architect*, January 1969)

The registration of 'good' designs in the Canadian 'Design Index' and the establishment of annual national design awards celebrated the work of the country's best
designers with congratulatory, sales-generating publicity. Department stores displayed winning products in their windows with the 'Design Award' label, a jaunty
triangular 'tick,' and manufacturers launched advertising campaigns highlighting
their recent awards. National magazines, daily newspapers, and weekend newspaper
supplements featured photographs of winning designs and designers. *Canadian Art*
reported that it had received inquiries about the 'Design Index' and requests from
England, France, Italy, and Australia to reprint photographs, while the Design
Centre was handling hundreds of requests annually for pamphlets and photographs.
Educational film-strips were available for schools and colleges and for retail staff-
training programs. Copies of the 'Design Index' publications were distributed to
public libraries. Even a motion picture was reported to be in the works, in late 1955,
that would 'explain in direct terms the relation of good product design to comfort
and convenience in the home.'[4]

In 1960, the National Industrial Design Council (NIDC) adopted a new policy
for the 'Design Index,' acknowledging only products, such as Court Noxon's new
steel tub chair (fig. 196), that were designed and made in Canada. Previously, any
goods manufactured in Canada had been eligible, even if designed elsewhere. This
anomaly had contributed to an odd scene in a retrospective exhibition organized by
the NIDC. Nine Canadian-designed armchairs and dining chairs were arranged in a
modest, neighbourly long line on the floor facing a single American chair, designed
by Charles Eames, which hovered on a suspended platform several feet above them.

The nature of official design advocacy was changed by the Industrial Design
Act of 1961, which established the National Design Branch of the federal Department
of Trade and Commerce, as well as a seventeen-member Design Council. In 1963
these two bodies were taken over by a new ministry simply called the Department of
Industry. These events amounted to a transfer of political responsibilty for design,
from culture to commerce.[5]

In the spirit of the new political agenda, a furniture trade mission was sent to
Europe that summer on behalf of Canadian manufacturers. Seven men, representing
government and industry, visited Britain, Denmark, Sweden, West Germany, and
Italy, making contact with foreign manufacturers and retailers through Canadian
trade-commission offices. The group investigated sources of raw materials, levels of
productivity, methods of management, design development, and marketing. Their
chief aim was to increase exports to these countries, while devising strategies to
fend off imports.[6]

Fig. 196 Armchair: steel tube, upholstery. Designed
by Court Noxon, Toronto. Manufactured by Metalsmiths,
Toronto (Metalsmiths catalogue)

The trade mission's report was released five months after the trip. It was summarized in the trade publication *Furniture and Furnishings* by editor Ben Fiber, who had been a member of the mission.[7] He was particularly impressed by the situation in Denmark, where there was no need for aggressive, expensive marketing because of the country's elevated level of design consciousness. Danish high-school students, Fiber reported, were taught interior decorating and furniture design and, along with other members of the public, were encouraged to enter design competitions. Original ideas could also be submitted to the various producers' unions which represented the country's large number of small craft and cabinet shops. The presentation of new lines of furniture by well-known designers was guaranteed to generate national debate.

In England, meanwhile, the furniture industry was 'muddling with the problem of converting from a craft industry to a [production] line industry.' Fiber thought that tax relief and low-cost federal loans would enable Canadian manufacturers to tackle a similar situation in Canada by modernizing plants to boost production and sales efficiency. Combined with government promotion and lower retail mark-ups, this formula might 'jigsaw into a grand scheme that would make the furniture industry the model of secondary manufacture in Canada.'

Fiber warned, as had others before him, that Canada needed more designers and better design in order to be able to export its furniture, and noted that the aspect of furniture promotion which most clearly distinguished European countries from Canada was their use of permanent craft and design exhibitions. He thought that the prestigious displays of Europe, in permanent design departments of public art galleries and museums, were more influential and commercially effective than Ottawa's 'industry sustaining experiments' limited to small-scale, temporary exhibitions and manufacturer's promotions.

Nevertheless, the federal government opened its second design centre, in 1964, in a prestigious shopping location on Bloor Street in Toronto. Two years later, another centre was opened, in an equally good location in Place Bonaventure in Montreal. Based on the Ottawa model, the design centres shared a modest retail sensibility in the scale and style of displays. They showed temporary exhibitions of Canadian and international design, with the focus on stylish home living. There were various public education programs, and local office and store workers were encouraged to treat the centres as reliable sources of product information and referrals. At the opening of the Toronto Design Centre, C.M. Drury, minister of industry, declared that 'this must be our goal, to gain an increasing reputation for the character of our goods and to set the cash registers of Canada ringing.'

In a luncheon speech at a Furniture Manufacturers' Management Day at the Royal York Hotel in Toronto, in July 1965, a Hudson's Bay Company executive told his audience that the babies of the postwar years were now turning up as customers. They were, he said, a 'sophisticated army of young people,' and he suggested that a good way for manufacturers to communicate directly with them would be to attach helpful information tags to the furniture. He also made the astute suggestion that, if manufacturers couldn't find the designers they needed in Canada, they should import them from other places. 'It is better to do this,' he explained, 'than to import their products from other countries.'

The Canadian National Exhibition in Toronto upgraded its level of design promotion with the Better Living Centre, opened in 1962. This 21,000-square-foot exhibition space was devoted to home furnishings and appliances, mainly from Canadian factories. The official program promised that 'every visitor to the CNE will find amazement and pleasure in exploring this remarkable building,' while that year's annual report declared that the 'fabulous new Better Living Centre ... awed the public.'

The annual manufacturers' trade show, the Canadian Furniture Mart, was held in the new centre, and in 1964 the show's organizers set up their own design council to adjudicate design awards and to promote design innovation. These lofty publicized aims were soon deflated by the show's own promotion, with the furniture on display becoming a backdrop – often a completely obscured backdrop – for young female models hired to pose for store buyers and newspaper photographers. Press reviews of the design-awards ceremony for the 1968 Furniture Mart listed all the fashion models, entertainers, and celebrities present before giving the names of the award winners. Long gone were the days when British art historian Herbert Read could be seriously proposed as a speaker for a Canadian manufacturers' convention, let alone a Mrs Pankhurst.

A more thorough and engaging approach to design advocacy was demonstrated in the pages of *Canadian Interiors*, a trade magazine for interior designers, started in 1964. Under the editorship of David Piper, *Canadian Interiors* made a consistently strong effort to present Canadian design in an informative way, mixing local and national coverage with international products and news. There were even occasional light-hearted nods to the anti-establishment/anti-design movement of the late 1960s. In one article, the West Coast architect and designer Peter Cotton reported the visual delight he had found in a local 'hip pad.' The living room was furnished with shabby, overstuffed armchairs and decorated with posters, mirrored mosaics, and old advertising signs. 'This room,' according to Cotton, 'had a presence, an immediacy which was of our time and spirit. The colors, forms, textures, and space were handled with a skill and a wit I admired.'[8] More radical design protests were not so easily assimilated. In October 1968, *Canadian Interiors* reported, with the brevity of disbelief, on the 14th Milan Triennale, closed by militant students one hour after it was officially opened.

Public, professional, and civic appreciation of contemporary furniture lagged behind parallel interests in architecture and city planning. The City of Toronto sponsored an international design competition for a new city hall in 1958, following the precedent set for the previous city hall, opened in 1891, also the result of an open design competition. The winning design in the new competition was by Finnish architect Viljo Revell and, upon its completion in 1965, his city hall met with enthusiastic critical and popular acclaim. The success of the project invigorated the architectural profession in Canada and advanced the cause of urban design in North American city centres. The process for the selection of furniture for the building, however, demonstrated no such commitment to excellence. In fact, the furnishing of Toronto City Hall became the country's first, and to date only, public furniture scandal.

City Council initially agreed to commission architect Revell's furniture designs, but then baulked at paying his professional design fees and decided instead to sponsor a local 'competition.' The city hired interior designer Alison Bain to redo Revell's space planning and then established a selection committee consisting of Professor Eric Arthur of the University of Toronto School of Architecture; Jack Mar, of John B. Parkin and Associates (representing Revell); Howard Chapman, of Chapman and Hurst architects; furniture designer Robin Bush; and interior designer Budd Sugarman. The committee conducted the process, not as an open design competition, but as a limited call for proposals. City administrators narrowed the field somewhat by requiring each competitor to submit a million-dollar performance bond. Five firms were eventually announced to be in the running, although one withdrew at the first hint of 'a political hassle.'[9] This left Knoll International Canada; Eaton's; Simpson's; and Sunar, a Canadian manufacturer.

These official 'competitors' were announced on 2 November 1964, but it was not until 19 January 1965, when they were more than halfway to their deadline, that the designers were given the official budget for the furniture: $850,000. At the beginning of April 1965, the selection committee announced that Knoll was the winner of the design competition. Shortly after, it was revealed that the cost of the Knoll proposal was $150,000 over budget. Knoll trimmed its price, twice, to just under the $850,000 limit, but the city's Board of Control eventually decided that Knoll had automatically disqualified itself by not originally sticking to the budget. Against the strong opposition of Mayor Philip Givens, the Board of Control decided to ignore the design competition completely and tried to award the tender to the lowest bidder, the Robert Simpson Company.

Chaos ensued. The lack of articulated objectives and professional controls for all stages of the competition process was now evident. Competitors had each received $5,000 as their official budget for design development, but no spending limits or standard presentation formats had been established. As a result, three of the teams spent between $35,000 and $45,000 on the preparation and presentation of their proposals. Knoll spent $60,000, twelve times the 'budget.' Bain's space planning was apparently never seen by any of the competitors, who were nevertheless bombarded with subsequent appendices to lists of requirements.[10]

The local media became involved, with *The Telegram* newspaper waging a vigorous campaign against Knoll, and warning City Council that it 'must choose between ethics and aesthetics.' Howard Chapman, a member of the selection committee, wrote to the press, complaining about the endless stream of misleading and inaccurate reports. One councillor declared during a council-chamber debate that 'people in glass houses shouldn't throw furniture,' and another challenged the mayor to explain 'this feeling' he had that the Knoll proposal was the best. Mayor

Givens replied: 'Why, I find it beautiful ... this is very hard to do. It would be like explaining love to you ... It sends me ... It grabs me ... I mean, it moves me.'[11]

At the council meeting of 15 April, there was a 10–10 deadlock in a vote on the acceptance of the Knoll proposal. After one councillor left the council chambers, the mayor again made a motion on the issue, and this time Knoll won by 10–9. On 2 June however, the Board of Control voted again to give the contract to Simpson's. As Robert Gretton pointed out in that month's issue of *Canadian Architect*, the problem had reached a point where it could bounce back and forth 'in perpetuum' between Board of Control and Council.

Controller Herbert Orliffe belatedly announced that 'the City should have had a design contest, picked a winner, and then called for tenders on the basis of the winning design.' It was too late to start over, however, and through pressure from the mayor and the selection committee, Knoll was eventually awarded the furniture contract for the new city hall. Knoll International Canada's director of design, John Quigg, supervised the project, using standard Knoll products and some custom-made pieces intended to reflect the architectural spirit of the building.

The contract-furniture market grew rapidly during the building boom of the 1960s, and sales competition within the industry was intense. Manufacturers were often accused of stealing designs from freelance designers, as well as from each other. In 1965, Cimon Limited, a Quebec manufacturer, successfully sued Bench Made Furniture for copying a sofa designed for Cimon by Luigi Tiengo. But few such cases reached court. Most, like the Toronto City Hall furniture 'competition,' became the bases of long-running, slow-burning disputes.

Expo 67 was Canada's first world's fair and an important national event which left a lasting effect on its host city, Montreal. Canadian families drove to Quebec from all over the country to share in the excitement, and the fair was celebrated as a great popular success. Expo 67, according to the weekly newsmagazine *The Canadian*, provided Canadian designers with 'a vast demand for their services and an unequalled showplace for their work.'[12]

Two dozen furniture manufacturers were scheduled to be invited to furnish model apartments in Habitat, the futuristic apartment building at Expo designed by Montreal architect Moishe Safdie. When designer Jacques Guillon found out about this plan, he persuaded the organizers to cut that list in half, and to give the other model apartments to independent interior designers and furniture designers. As there were no funds available for design or fabrication, the designers had to make their own arrangements with local manufacturers and craftspeople to provide the furnishings needed.

Guillon and his associates, who had designed the carriage seating for Montreal's new Métro, produced large laminated-oak armchairs and moulded-ply-wood dining chairs that could be easily disassembled for shipping. Knock-down ply-wood furniture was also shown by Robert Kaiser. His tables, chairs, beds, and storage units were manufactured by Takna, using unusual wood stains in orange, blue, green, and white. Interior designer Alison Hymas, an Albertan graduate of the University of Manitoba, designed boxy seating units in oak-veneered plywood inspired by the cubic shapes of the Habitat building itself. A team from the Toronto firm of Dudas Kuypers Rowan, headed by Jerry Adamson, designed moulded-plastic chairs and ottomans of polyethylene, left bare for outdoor use or covered with a thin layer of foam and upholstery fabric for indoors (figs. 197 and 198). These were accompanied by tables of moulded Fibreglas or sheet acrylic. One suite was done by Chris Sorensen, of Montreal, who had studied furniture and upholstery design in Copenhagen before immigrating to Canada. Others were designed by Keith Muller and Michael Stewart, and by architect Macy DuBois, all of Toronto.

The editor of *Canadian Homes*, Harris Mitchell, thought that the furniture made for Habitat 'showed a proud confidence in the Canadian capacity to produce' and that it represented a 'bold leap into a whole new concept of design and production' (fig. 199).[13] According to Alison Hymas, the huge gap between the designers' model apartments and the manufacturers' was 'the best advertisement' for professional design imaginable.[14]

An energetic optimism was evident throughout Expo 67, and the fair was widely promoted as the international debut of professional Canadian design. Interest in industrial design was reported to be strong among the general public and the business community. Ontario, still the centre of the Canadian furniture-manufacturing industry, sponsored a furniture competition called 'Design '67.' The following year, the province's Department of Trade and Development initiated the Eedee Awards for furniture design. These introduced many new designers to the industry (figs. 200 and 201), including several graduates of the Furniture Programme at Ryerson Institute of Technology in Toronto, in particular the prolific Thomas Lamb (figs. 202 and 203). In 1969, the Interior Decorators Society of Quebec started its own annual design awards for residential and commercial furniture, and at the end of 1970 the federal government announced a new business-oriented award, the National Design Council Chairman's Award for Design Management.

But Expo 67 seemed to exhaust the country's energy and imagination. Design success was widely assumed to be a fact, accomplished by the mere fulfilment of the event itself. The sheer scale of the Montreal fair pre-empted the demand for more modest programs and, perhaps as a result, design exhibitions virtually disappeared from public museums and art galleries. Government support for design advocacy faltered, and official overseas promotion of Canadian products was erratic and uninspired. At an international design exhibition and trade fair in Copenhagen, a city of design excellence, in January 1968, just months after Expo, Canada was represented by a small booth stocked with shopping bags, books of matches, and maps of Canada.[15]

The Design Council showed signs of malaise. Its 'Design Index' project was gradually turning into an unmanageable and unusable collection of documents and photographs, because the input process was allowed to become one of automatic, rather than selective, registration. This undermined the program's original purpose

Fig. 197 Moulded-polypropylene out-door seating. Designed by Dudas Kuypers Rowan, Toronto. Model apartment at Habitat, Expo 67, Montreal (*The Canadian Architect*, October 1967)

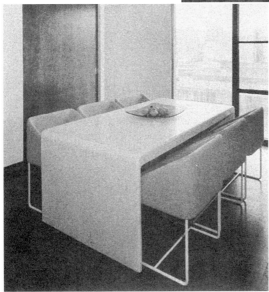

Fig. 198 Dining room designed by Dudas Kuypers Rowan, Toronto, for Habitat model apartment, Expo 67, Montreal (*The Canadian Architect*, October 1967)

Fig. 199 Outdoor chair: aluminum tube, vinyl. Designed by Michel D'Allaire for Jacques Guillon and Associates, Montreal. Manufactured by Paul Arno, Montreal, 1967. Displayed at Habitat, Expo 67 (Canadian Product Design poster, published by Design Canada, Ottawa 1968, for the Milan Triennale)

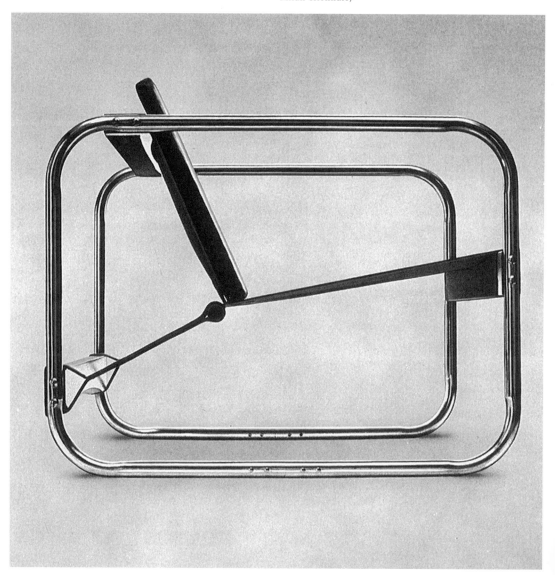

Fig. 200 MS stacking chair: moulded plywood, laminated wood. Designed by Keith Muller and Michael Stewart, Toronto, 1968. Manufactured by Ambiant Systems Limited, Toronto (Photo: Ambiant Systems)

Fig. 201 Armchair: aluminum tube, fabric. Designed by Al Faux, Toronto, 1967 (*Canadian Architect*, January 1969)

Fig. 202 Folding garden chairs:
aluminum tube, canvas. Designed by
Thomas Lamb, Toronto, 1969 (Photo:
Thomas Lamb)

Fig. 203 Garden seating: stamped metal and metal tube. Designed by Thomas Lamb, Toronto, 1967. Made by Bunting, USA (Photo: Thomas Lamb)

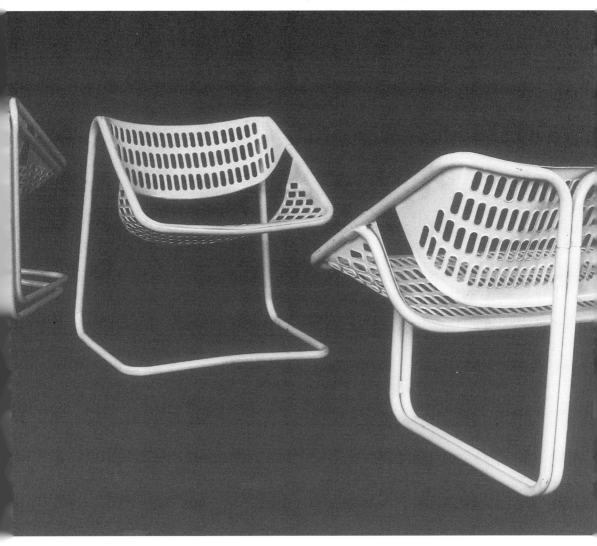

Fig. 204 Cocktail table: white PVC tubing. Designed and made by Donald Lloyd McKinley, director of furniture studio, Sheridan College School of Design, Mississauga, Ontario, 1969 (Photo: Donald McKinley)

Fig. 205 Table and stool: moulded plastic. Designed by Aldo and Francesco Piccaluga, Toronto, 1970. Manufactured by Synthesis, Toronto (Photo: Aldo and Francesco Piccaluga, Architects)

Fig. 206 Stool: bent steel tube, bent steel sheet. Designed by Philip Salmon and Hugh Hamilton, Toronto, 1970. Manufactured by Kinetics Furniture, Toronto (Photo: Kinetics)

and value. In an incident indicative of the lack of conscientious leadership, the head of the Design Council, E.P. Weiss, told a reporter during a 1968 phone interview that his department had given out its annual design scholarships, but he did not know how many, how much, or to whom.[16]

It was the high-profile design centres in Toronto and Montreal, however, that first came under official scrutiny. The federal government commissioned John B. Parkin, architect and ex-president of the Association of Canadian Industrial Designers, to conduct a study of their effectiveness, including their cost-effectiveness. Based on his recommendation, both centres were closed in 1970. Many industrial designers objected to this drastic action. Some suggested that the design centres could simply be moved to less expensive locations. Everyone, including Parkin and the government, was in agreement that all the design centres had been well managed and that their exhibitions, seminars, and lectures had been popular with designers and the general public. And no one disputed the value of the new work being done by Canadian designers (figs. 204–6).

The design centres were still administered by the National Design Council, whose chairman was Parkin's professional associate John C. Parkin. According to the council, which was now part of the federal Department of Industry, Trade, and Commerce, the design centres had increased consumer awareness of design issues, their primary goal, but had not had the desired impact on the manufacturing sector.

The council did not explain its parameters for efficacy in this regard, or its reasons for refusing cheaper operating options. Government funding previously devoted to the centres' public activities was now transferred to direct support for industry initiatives. This shift was implemented through the Industrial Design Assistance Programme, which benefited specific new industries such as aerospace, but did not contribute in any way to developing commercial markets for designed goods and design culture.

The federal government's commitment to design promotion was apparently insufficient to support both types of programs. The closing of the design centres was not due to any perceived failure in the fulfilment of their public-education and promotion mandate. It was, instead, the result of a lapse in the political will to sponsor a comprehensive plan of effective design advocacy. Ottawa's politicians and bureaucrats, along with their architect-advisers, were apparently unable to initiate bold, entertaining strategies for the 1970s, in step with the effervescent energy of the times.

The educational infrastructure, industrial incentives, and cultural initiatives needed for sustained progress in furniture design and production were still erroneously regarded in Canada as divergent, even conflicting, priorities. For most manufacturers, bankers, and curators, the obvious, everyday links between aesthetic exploration and economic expansion, and between critical commentary and consumer consciousness, remained unnecessarily obscure.

Notes

Chapter 1 Introduction from Europe

1 *Industrial Canada*, published by the Canadian Manufacturers' Association, February 1922.

2 "Boosting Business with a Baby Clinic,' *The Grand Rapids Furniture Record*, April 1923.

3 Arthur Pulos, *American Design Ethic* (Cambridge, MA: MIT Press, 1983).

4 *The Industrial Arts*, published by Department of Overseas Trade, Britain, 1925.

5 Press clippings in correspondence files of the Exhibition Branch, Department of Immigration and Colonization, Ottawa. Public Archives.

6 Correspondence, Exhibition Branch, Department of Immigration and Colonization, Ottawa. Public Archives.

7 Anne Elizabeth Wilson, "Spring Fabrics and What to Do with Them,' *Canadian Homes and Gardens,* April 1926.

8 James Acton, *Book of Canadian Furniture* (Toronto: Acton Publishers, 1923). Metropolitan Toronto Reference Library, Special Collections.

9 Acton's list is not complete, and might be a trade directory in which manufacturers paid to be listed. For example, he does not list the Valley City Seating Company, in Dundas, Ontario, which made folding chairs for assembly halls, or George B. Meadows Limited, in Toronto, manufacturer of office furniture since 1854.

10 *The Canadian Hotel Review* (Toronto: Fisher Publishing Company, March 1928).

11 *The Grand Rapids Furniture Record*, January 1921.

12 Publicity files of the Robert Simpson Company, the Hudson's Bay Company Archives.

13 'A Dining Room in the New Manner,' *Canadian Homes and Gardens*, April 1928.

14 Alice Mackay, 'Rideau Hall Interprets the Oriental Mood,' *Canadian Homes and Gardens*, February 1927.

15 Alice M. Cooper, 'Some Modernizing Notes in Color,' *Canadian Homes and Gardens*, April 1927.

16 Alice M. Cooper, 'Characteristics of Modernism in Interior Decoration,' *Canadian Homes and Gardens*, November 1928.

17 'A New Chapter in English Furniture,' *Canadian Homes and Gardens*, April 1928.

18 Mary-Etta Macpherson, 'When Old Traditions and New Forms Meet,' *Canadian Homes and Gardens,* September 1928.

19 These were designed by A.F. Harvey, of Toronto, and made by Mark Smith, of the John Lindsay Company, also in Toronto.

20 Estelle Burke (article on lighting), *Canadian Homes and Gardens*, November 1928.

21 *Chatelaine*, February 1930.

22 Mary-Etta Macpherson, 'The Canadian House of Today,' *Canadian Homes and Gardens*, June 1929.

23 Henry Morgan and Company advertisement, *Montreal Gazette*, 20 November 1925.

24 *Canadian Homes and Gardens*, February 1929.

25 *Books on Furniture*, Grand Rapids Public Library, December 1927.

26 *Canadian Homes and Gardens*, January 1929.

27 Ibid., February 1929.

28 James Cowan, *Maclean's Magazine,* 15 May 1929.

29 *The Canadian Hotel Review*, Royal York Souvenir Number, July 1929 (Toronto: Fisher Publishing Company).

30 Lovely Linen advertisement, *Canadian Homes and Gardens*, 1930.

31 Included in this estimate are *The RAIC Journal, Canadian Homes and Gardens, Mayfair, Maclean's Magazine, The Montreal Gazette,* and *The Globe and Mail.*

Chapter 2 The Furniture Professions

1 *Nos intérieurs de demain* (Montreal: Librairie d'Action Canadienne-Française Limitée 1929.)

2 'The Allied Arts at the Recent Toronto Chapter Exhibition,' *Journal of the Royal Architectural Institute of Canada [RAIC Journal],* May 1927.

3 The exhibition included a wrought-iron fire-screen by the renowned firm of Edgar Brandt, of Paris and New York.

4 E.H. Blake, 'The New Interest in Architecture,' *RAIC Journal,* May 1931. (The situation did improve greatly; see fig. 99.)

5 W.L. Somerville, 'Is Our Domestic Architecture Mediocre?,' ibid., April 1932.

6 W.L. Somerville, 'Why Modern?,' ibid., January–February 1938.

7 'Decoration Arts,' *Canadian Homes and Gardens,* January–February 1936.

8 *Canadian Art,* Summer 1945. It is not clear whether this means 5,000 pieces or 5,000 different designs, including all catalogue and custom items.

9 'Niches Lined with Mirrors Might Work the Transformation' (Eaton's advertisement), *Canadian Homes and Gardens,* March 1933.

10 Standard Tube Company advertisement, ibid., June 1931.

11 Snyder's also had a factory in Montreal at this time and employed more than 400 people (conversation with the Snyder family, Waterloo, 1985). Many American products were also available just about everywhere in Canada. The Kroehler Manufacturing Company, for example, in the mid-1930s, had Canadian plants at Stratford and Montreal, in addition to seven plants in the United States.

12 At the end of the 1930s, the society again had only ten 'active members': Laurence Barraud, C. John Carter, Minerva Elliot, Augusta Fleming, Anne Harris, Robert Irvine, Freda James, Mina Saxe, and R. Malcolm Slimon, all of Toronto, and Donald Rutledge, of London.

13 Julius Meier-Graefe, the socialist Belgian design critic and proprietor of the first modern decorative-arts gallery, 'Modern Age,' in Paris, 1899.

14 *Canadian Homes and Gardens,* February 1934.

15 *RAIC Journal,* April 1937.

16 Beginning in 1932, exhibition spaces were made available to exhibitors at a rental fee not exceeding 50 per cent of the cost to the Canadian government.

17 Canadian decorative arts were represented in this pavilion by the work of New Brunswick potters Karl and Erica Deichmann, who gave demonstrations of throwing and glazing.

18 The arm on the armchair and sofa of the 'Interchangeable Modern' line by Saarinen for Imperial in 1941 is the same as the arm on one of Russell Wright's 'Modern Maple' armchairs for Snyder's in 1936.

19 Jean-Marie Gauvreau, *Evolution et tradition des meubles canadiens* (Ottawa: La Société Royale du Canada, 1944).

Chapter 3 Craft and Design

1 'Some Aspects of Our Wartime Controls,' *Industrial Canada,* July 1944.

2 If Thrift's view was correct, then the manufacturing situation had somehow regressed since the 1920s, when Globe Furniture, of Waterloo, was making compound curved-plywood seating, and the early 1930s, when many manufacturers were using bent solid wood and bent metal tube and sheet. It is likely that sufficient technical expertise would have been available for profitable experimentation within the Ontario industry, if trained designers had been available to provide guidance.

3 *Canadian Homes and Gardens*, June 1945

4 'Does Contemporary Design Mean Anything to You?' *Canadian Homes and Gardens*, June 1945.

5 *Canadian Art*, Summer 1945.

6 'The Importance of Design in Industry,' *Industrial Canada*, July 1945.

7 *Industrial Canada*, February 1946.

8 In October of the same year, the gallery hosted a design exhibition from the MOMA titled 'If You Want to Build a House.'

9 'Reconstruction and Economic Development Conference,' *Industrial Canada*, July 1946.

10 The reason for the refusal of the patent is not known to this author.

11 From John Neuhart, Marilyn Neuhart, and Ray Eames, *Eames Design: The Work of the Office of Charles and Ray Eames* (New York: Harry N. Abrams, 1989). Eames worked on this project with members of the Engineering Faculty at the University of California, Los Angeles.

12 Donald W. Buchanan, *Design for Use in Canadian Products* (Ottawa: National Gallery of Canada, in cooperation with the Department of Reconstruction and Supply and the National Film Board of Canada, January 1947).

13 Ven-Rez Products still manufactures plywood and metal furniture in Shelburne.

14 'Coast to Coast in Art: Design in Industry,' *Canadian Art,* November 1946.

15 Donald Buchanan, 'Take Another Look at Your Kitchen Range,' *Canadian Art*, Spring/Summer 1948.

16 F.S. Haines, 'A New School of Design,' *Canadian Art*, Summer 1945.

17 Donald Buchanan, 'The Canadian Picture,' *RAIC Journal*, July 1947.

18 *Canadian Art*, November 1945.

19 Ibid., Christmas–New Year 1949–50.

20 As of writing, in 1996, university-level professional training for craftspeople in Canada is available in only two of the ten provinces, Quebec and Nova Scotia.

21 Advertisement in *Canadian Art*, 1949.

22 'Canadian Art Schools,' *Canadian Art*, Summer 1947.

Chapter 4 Architects and Advocacy

1 Now the Albright–Knox Museum. The project, which consisted of design index, monograph, and exhibition, was organized by the Buffalo Fine Arts Academy of the Albright Art Gallery, and sponsored by the Gaylord Container Corporation, of St Louis, Missouri.

2 This collection is now owned by the National Gallery, in Washington, DC.

3 Peter Day, 'The Future That Can Be Ours,' in Peter Day and Linda Lewis, *Art in Everyday Life* (Toronto: Summerhill Press/The Power Plant, 1988).

4 Ibid.

5 Donald Buchanan, 'Design Index,' *Canadian Art*, Christmas 1947.

6 The Eames chairs were not yet available in Canada, but Aalto plywood furniture from Finland was sold at the time by Eaton's.

7 *The Story Behind the Design Centre* (Ottawa: The National Gallery of Canada, 1955).

8 Donald Buchanan, 'Design in Industry,' *Industrial Canada*, July 1946.

9 'These Are the Ones the Experts Picked,' *Canadian Art,* Spring 1949.

10 'Western Canada Views Designs for Everyday Use,' *Canadian Art*, October 1949.

11 'Increased Support for Industrial Designers,' *Canadian Art*, Autumn 1948. The names of the four schools and five students are not given.

12 *Design for Living*, catalogue published by the Community Arts Council and the Vancouver Art Gallery, 1949.

13 Scott Watson, 'Art in the Fifties,' *Vancouver: Art and Artists,1931–1983* (Vancouver: Vancouver Art Gallery, 1983).

14 *Canadian Homes and Gardens*, January–July, 1950

Chapter 5 Committees,
Competitions, and Commissions

1 Donald Buchanan, 'Introducing Manu-facturers to Designers,' *Canadian Art,* Christmas–New Year, 1949–50.

2 'A Report on the Designing of Canadian Furniture,' *Canadian Art,* Autumn 1950.

3 In 1950, Snyder's of Waterloo was the only Canadian manufacturer whose entire product line was modern.

4 Robert Fones [curator], *A Spanner in the Works: The Furniture of Russell Spanner, 1950–1953,* exhibition catalogue (Toronto: The Power Plant, 1990).

5 *Canadian Art,* October 1951.

6 A Thonet catalogue, *ca* 1933–4, includes a photograph of sixteen Thonet workers standing on a dining table. Derek E. Ostergard, ed., *Bent Wood and Metal Furniture: 1850–1946* (Seattle: The University of Washington Press, and The American Federation of Arts, 1987).

7 In his exhibition catalogue, Fones explains that this name probably came from the Originals Club, an Elm Street bar frequented by Spanner, his friends, and co-workers: *A Spanner in the Works.*

8 Ibid.

9 Alec Winter, retailer, in conversation with the author, Toronto, 1985.

10 'A Report on the Designing of Canadian Furniture,' *Canadian Art,* Autumn 1950.

11 *Canadian Homes and Gardens,* June 1951.

12 Allan Collier [curator], *West Coast Modern,* exhibition catalogue (Vancouver: Vancouver Art Gallery, 1988).

13 Ibid.

14 According to the *Canadian Homes and Gardens* caption, two members of this team were named Hugh McMillan.

15 Adolf Loos, 'Furniture for Sitting,' Vienna, 1898, in *Spoken into the Void: Collected Essays, 1897–1900,* trans. Jane O. Newman and John H. Smith (Cambridge, MA: MIT Press, 1982).

16 *Design (U.K.),* no. 27, 1951.

17 Humphrey Carver, 'The Design Centre – The First Year,' *Canadian Art,* Spring 1954.

18 'Promoting Canadian Design,' *Design (U.K.),* no. 56, 1953.

Chapter 6 Design Issues

1 'Canada Participates in the X Triennale,' *Canadian Art,* New Year 1955.

2 Calvert also worked as a home-planning consultant for *Canadian Homes and Gardens,* and later directed landscape architecture for Expo 67. From notes provided by Allan Collier, 1993.

3 Alec Winter, a retailer with sixty years' experience, in the Modern Age stores and elsewhere. In conversation with the author, 1985.

4 'Canadian Art on Television,' *Canadian Art,* October 1952.

5 *RAIC Journal,* December 1954.

6 All of this furniture was made by the Toronto manufacturer Leif Jacobsen.

7 *Canadian Art,* Spring 1955. Mrs W.F. Harrison, of the Canadian Association of Consumers, pointed to inconsistencies in the other speakers' comments. Some stated that 'the consumers are the persons who dictate what the manufacturer is to make,' while others insisted that the consumers 'don't know what they are looking for.'

8 *Canadian Homes and Gardens,* September 1958.

9 Ibid.

10 Warnett Kennedy, 'Industrial Design,' in Malcolm Rosss, ed., *The Arts in Canada: A Stocktaking at Mid-Century* (Toronto: Macmillan, 1958).

Chapter 7 In The Spotlight

1 T.C. Wood, 'Designing the Exhibits: A Three-Year Project,' *Canadian Art,* August 1958.

2 D. Buchanan, 'Impressions of the Fair,' *Canadian Art,* August 1958.

3 David Piper, 'Stefan Siwinski,' *Canadian Interiors*, 1971.

4 *The Story behind the Design Centre* (Ottawa: National Industrial Design Council and The National Gallery, 1955).

5 This was pointed out by Peter Day in his essay 'The Future that Can Be Ours' in Peter Day and Linda Lewis, *Art in Everyday Life*, exhibition catalogue (Toronto: Summerhill Press/The Power Plant, 1988).

6 'Furniture Mission to Europe,' *Furniture and Furnishings*, June 1963. The group included the designer Jan Kuypers.

7 Ben Fiber, 'A Report to the Industry,' *Furniture and Furnishings*, November 1963.

8 Peter Cotton, 'The Hip Pad,' *Canadian Interiors*, December 1968.

9 'What Went On,' *Canadian Interiors*, July 1965.

10 Ibid.

11 'The Great Furniture Debate,' *The Canadian Architect*, June 1965.

12 Harris Mitchell, 'What's New in Furniture?' *Canadian Homes*, in *The Canadian*, September 1967.

13 Ibid.

14 Alison Hymas, in conversation with the author, 1993.

15 Bernadette Andrews, 'An Open Letter to Mr. Drury,' *Canadian Interiors*, January 1968.

16 Ibid.

Bibliography

Canadian Architect. Toronto, 1955–.

Canadian Art. Toronto, 1943–66.

Canadian Homes, In *The Canadian*. Toronto, 1960–70

Canadian Homes and Gardens. Toronto: The Maclean Publishing Company Limited, 1924–60.

Canadian Interiors. Toronto, 1964–90.

Chamberlain, K.E. *Design in Canada, 1940–1987: A Bibliography*. Richmond, BC: K.E. Chamberlain, 1988.

Collier, Allan. *West Coast Modern*. Exhibition catalogue. Vancouver: The Vancouver Art Gallery, 1988.

Day, Peter, and Linda Lewis. *Art in Everyday Life*. Exhibition catalogue. Toronto: Summerhill Press/ The Power Plant, 1988.

Decorative Arts annuals, 1920–70. London and New York: Studio Publications.

Design for Living. Exhibition catalogue. Vancouver: The Community Arts Council and The Vancouver Art Gallery, 1949.

Design, U.K. London, 1900–90.

École du Meuble, 1930–1950. Exhibition catalogue. Montreal: Château Dufresne, 1989.

Evolution et tradition des meubles canadiens. Ottawa: La Société Royale du Canada, 1944.

Fones, Robert. *A Spanner in the Works: The Furniture of Russell Spanner, 1950–1953*. Exhibition catalogue. Toronto: The Power Plant, 1990.

Furniture and Furnishings. Toronto: 1963–82.

The Grand Rapids Furniture Record. Grand Rapids, 1900–39.

Industrial Canada. Toronto: The Canadian Manufacturers' Association, 1900–73.

Industrial Design. New York: Whitney Publications, 1954–70.

McKaskell, Robert, Sandra Paikowsky, Allan Collier, and Virginia Wright. *Achieving the Modern: Canadian Abstract Painting and Design in the 1950s*. Exhibition catalogue. Winnipeg: Winnipeg Art Gallery, 1993.

Mayfair. Toronto: The Maclean Publishing Company, 1927–59.

Ontario Homes and Living. Vancouver: Mitchell Press Limited, 1962–6.

Royal Architectural Institute of Canada Journal. Ottawa: Royal Architectural Institute of Canada, 1924–60.

The Story behind the Design Centre. Ottawa: National Industrial Design Council and The National Gallery of Canada, 1955.

Watson, Scott. *Vancouver: Art and Artists, 1931–1983*. Exhibition catalogue. Vancouver: The Vancouver Art Gallery, 1983.

Western Homes and Living. Vancouver: Mitchell Press Limited, 1952–70.

Wright, Virginia. *Seduced and Abandoned: Modern Furniture Designers in Canada, The First Fifty Years*. Exhibition catalogue Toronto: The Art Gallery at Harbourfront, 1985.

Sources of Illustrations

Architecture Library, University of Manitoba
Art Gallery of Ontario Archives
Bibliothèque Nationale du Québec
British Columbia Archives
Canadian Architectural Archives, University of Calgary
Canadian Pacific Limited Archives
City of Toronto Archives
City of Vancouver Archives
Grand Rapids Public Library
Metropolitan Toronto Reference Library
National Archives of Canada
National Library of Canada
Ontario College of Art Archives
Provincial Archives of Manitoba
Provincial Archives of Ontario
Public Archives of Nova Scotia
Robarts Library, University of Toronto
Thomas Fisher Rare Book Library, University of Toronto
Vancouver Art Gallery Archives
Vancouver Public Library
Winnipeg Art Gallery

Index